Parenting Outside the Box

Parenting Outside the Box

Honoring the *Spirit* in Your Children

Diane Hawkins Summers

Parenting Outside the Box
Diane Hawkins Summers

Original editing by Becky Colgan
Designed by Communication Strategies
Finishing design by Ellen Goodwin
Photography by Heather Van Gaale, *www.blinkphoto.com*
Photo of author by Marla Moore
Cover design by Seannon P. Garriepy, *www.garriepydesigns.com*

Published by Summerville Spirit, Inc.
2345 Trails End
Fallbrook, CA 92028
(760) 728-3222

Building Relationships with Love

ISBN 0-9774866-0-5

    This book is designed to provide general information on parenting and child development. It is sold with the understanding that the publisher and author are not engaged in rendering specific advice or services.
    The purpose of this book is to educate and entertain. It is designed to complement, amplify, and supplement other texts. The reader is encouraged to read all of the available material, to learn as much as possible about parenting and child development, and to tailor the information to meet individual needs.
    Every effort has been made to make this book as complete and as accurate as possible. However, there may be mistakes in both typography and content. Therefore, this text should be used only as a general guide and not as the ultimate source of parenting or child development information. Furthermore, this book contains information current only up to the date of publication.

Dedicated to

Jim Hawkins

Your joy and humor will always be with me.

Table of Contents

Foreword ix

Acknowledgements xi

Introduction xiii

Chapter 1   Imagine 1

Chapter 2   Parenting Styles 11

Chapter 3   Parenting Partners 25

Chapter 4   Life Stages 35

Chapter 5   Discipline 43

Chapter 6   Learning 61

Chapter 7   Morals 75

Chapter 8   Health 97

Chapter 9   Traditions 117

Chapter 10   Gifts 125

Notes 139

Foreword

It is difficult to gauge the appealing quality of a book, in the face of changing tastes and fashion, even when the subject matter is one of such importance as parenting. One would imagine by the sheer enormity of the population who eventually find themselves as parents that there would be a plethora of books, and interest, in this subject. And, indeed, a trip to any local corner bookstore, community library, or mega-bookstore, with a stroll down the "Parenting" aisle, would easily convince most people of an overabundance of information available to young parents endeavoring to sort their way through parenthood. Add to this the constant bombardment from advice column writers, TV personalities, and even neighbors, and it's easy to understand why a certain state of confusion exists in the land of parenting today.

Against such a backdrop, why another book for parents? Or, what does this *Parenting Outside the Box* bring to the reader that may be lacking in the others? Simply put, there is still precious little an adult will accomplish in life that will compare with the experience of having raised a child from birth through adulthood. So, yes, while one could make a case that there are far too many books that tell us how to parent, unfortunately, there are far too few that focus, as does *Parenting Outside the Box*, on what being a parent is about. Moreover, there are far too few books of this genre that acknowledge the element of time in the parent and child relationship. In fact, the notion of time, and how we pay attention to it, weaves its way throughout this book as the author invites the reader to savor, to go slow, and to discuss as you proceed on your journey through not only this book but the spiritual awakening of both you and your child that parenthood brings.

Personally, during most of my childhood years, there was basically one source of help for parents, and that was Benjamin

Spock—although most parents of that generation would probably have had a hard time admitting to themselves that they were so inept as parents that they would have to seek advice from outside the family circle. Most parenting techniques at that time, in today's world, and regrettably for years to come, will for the most part consist of doing "what was done to us." As a consultant to families and educators, I would say that the spell of "what was done to us" is the biggest roadblock to establishing the kind of parent-and-child loving alliance that should exist universally.

So, dear reader, if you are wondering if you will come across words like effective, successful, complete or perfect in this book, be forewarned. Personally, I came away appreciating the author's candor about her own life and her experiences as a teacher and what that meant to her as she confronted changes in "tastes and fashion," or more appropriately stated in the jargon of parenting today—"practices." What there are here are real, practical, down-to-earth experiences the author has drawn from. We, as readers, benefit greatly from her own spiritual journey through life from daughter to college student, to classroom teacher, to college professor, and all along the way—mother. The scope of the author's knowledge guarantees that there is something here for everyone. It's a book to be read more than once. A book to flop open occasionally to help remind yourself that for all its trials and tribulations, there is nothing like being a parent to make one feel alive.

When I reached the end of this book, I realized my own rather cynical question had changed from "why did she need to write this book," to "it was inevitable that she should write it."

Michael Leeman
Education Consultant/Publisher
Turn the Page Press
Roseville, CA

Acknowledgments

This book is a compilation of experiences from an abundance of resources. It started as a legacy for my daughters, Sharri Guerrero and Amy Hawkins, several years ago. My nurse practitioner friend, Patricia Haase, encouraged me through my first draft. Joli Andre, a true lady of grace and etiquette, later mentored me. And my photographer, Heather Van Gaale, added her artistic talents.

Persons who kindly read the manuscript, giving great suggestions and comments, were: Chris Assad, Barbara Clark, Rich Collins, Michael Leeman, Sara Hernandez, Dr. Virginia (Ginger) Marable, and Jim Riordan. Endorsements from Dr. Joanna Payne-Jones, Dr. Becky Bailey, and Reverend Diane Harmony were greatly appreciated. But more than anyone else, great thanks goes to my husband, Reverend Michael Summers, for his endless devotion to this process. I am filled with gratitude for all the nurturing and love they have given me.

Introduction

Parenting Outside the Box will not teach you "how to parent," but rather "how to *be* a parent." The purpose of this book is to emphasize the responsibility of spiritual awakening for children. It addresses the parenting skills learned from the twentieth century and the challenges parents face in the twenty-first century. It is for people who are considering becoming parents, experienced parents, teachers, caregivers, and grandparents.

Parenting Outside the Box examines the question, What can families and communities do to positively nurture kids? Enjoy one chapter at a time with your parenting partners and support systems. Then discuss, debate, and decide the path you will take to support the next generation of children.

Peace and blessings.

Anything you can imagine is real.

~ *Pablo Picasso*

Twenty-four/Seven

When you're a parent, you do not get a whole night's sleep for about ten years.

When you're a parent, you carry a diaper bag instead of a purse.

When you're a parent, you watch "kid" TV for years and are oblivious to the world news.

When you're a parent, you walk around toys as if there were land mines all over your house.

When you're a parent, you live for at least one hour of quiet before you collapse into oblivion, which you used to know as sleep.

When you're a parent, going shopping for groceries or going to the mall with the kids is like being a drill sergeant in the Marine Corps.

The command mantra goes something like this: "Get in the car. Get out of the car. Do not run in the parking lot. Stay with me. No, you cannot eat that off of the floor."

When you're a parent, meals go something like this: "What do you want to eat? No, you cannot eat spaghetti for breakfast. Here is some Little Bunny Crunch cereal. Here, have some fruit. You won't eat the fruit. Here, I'll put your fruit in a smoothie for you."

When you're a parent, life is never boring. You are always washing clothes, picking up toys, bringing the kids here and there and attending about a zillion kid birthday parties.

When you're a parent, your true treasure is before your eyes every day.

When you're a parent, your life is as real as it will ever be.

When you're a parent, embrace life every day and be glad in it.

~D. H. Summers

Parenting Outside the Box

CHAPTER 1

Imagine

The Land of Chaos

The alarm clock rings. You notice you have overslept by twenty minutes. You go to make some coffee and realize there isn't any left. Your spouse is running around trying to get out of the house. Your teenager is refusing to get up. Your six-year-old cannot find her homework. Your three-year-old is crying because he wants his cereal right now. And you are close to being hysterical because you cannot find your car keys. If this is your typical morning, then get a grip. It's great that you are able to sit long enough to read this book. Congratulations! You must be on some long-deserved vacation in Hawaii. Well, maybe not. Nevertheless, learning about parenting is good. It means you are a responsible parent. However, it takes more than getting organized to be a good parent. Parenting requires you to look at your priorities. For example, you can decrease stress with meaningful dialogue. Let's examine how you can do this.

Are discussions in your household ever charged with emotion? Are expectations sometimes unclear for yourself and your children? Are fun family experiences few and far between? Does stress saturate any of your family situations? Do you feel you are just coping?

If you can answer yes to any of these questions, ask yourself, "What do I really want out of life?" If you want more than you have now, change lanes just like you would on the freeway. Make a shift. It does not have to be major. Just change lanes, not direction.

My Recipe for Parenting

I have been teaching child development for thirty years. During that time people have asked me, "What is the best way to raise kids?" The answer is, "You have to find your own way." Every parent takes what they experienced from their own childhood and combines it with what their parenting partner experienced. Then you may add a little parenting education by reading articles or books from the prevailing social consciousness. Bingo! You have parenting figured out. But there is more to it. Let's begin with a historical perspective.

Leaping from the Twentieth Century into the Twenty-First Century

In the early twentieth century, childhood as we know it today did not exist. People had a lot of children back then. The mortality rate for infants and young children was high. If they survived, they went to school (if they could) for a few years before going to work.

In the 1920s, women were allowed to vote, and children started going to school until they were eighteen. During World War II, women did the work of men on the home front, and young children started going to day care. In the 1960s, birth control gave women even more freedom, and children came home after school to empty houses—thus, the term *latchkey kids*. As mothers progressed in the professional world, so did children in *their* world.

Later in the century, standards for day care improved, public education expanded, and community and four-year colleges flourished. Now, in the beginning of the twenty-first century, we have exceptional education for everyone. Or do we? Some people argue that life today has too much—too much work, too much education, and not enough time for quality family life. They want to go back to the days of *Little House on the Prairie*. I don't agree. I believe that high-quality family life is not only possible, but also a necessary manifestation of the new century. You should expect to have superior educational experiences for your children as well as wonderful family experiences, especially because of the abundant time in which you live. The following five steps, which are explained further in this book, will help:

1. Examine your own childhood with forgiveness and gratitude (Chapter 1)

2. Consciously plan your parenting style (Chapter 2)

3. Promote a healthy learning environment (Chapters 3, 4, 5, and 6)

4. Be an example of good morals (Chapter 7)

5. Enjoy the process (Chapters 9 and 10)

My Childhood Perspective of Parenting

In 1958, when I was twelve years old, my family moved to California from Chicago. We spent six days driving on Route 66. I can remember, as we approached San Bernardino, how excited I was to see my first palm trees.

After moving in and getting settled, my sister, brother, and I really wanted to see the beach. Almost six months went by before we got our chance. My father got home from work a little early one day and, since it was daylight savings time, off we went. He picked up a six-pack of beer along the way to the beach. My sister, brother, and I could hardly contain our excitement. We ran to the water and gathered seashells. When we proudly showed our parents the precious collection, they both laughed and said, "Oh, that's nice." As soon as the beer was gone, we headed home.

Okay, I thought to myself. I guess this is all we are going to get for family outings—and I was right. We never went back to the beach, to a park, or even out for pizza.

As I made friends in the neighborhood, I went to the beach with their families. We left early in the day. We brought food, blankets, and wore our swimsuits. We swam. We stayed late and drove home tired and satisfied. When I went to the beach with my friends' families, it was a totally different experience. It was *quality family time*.

I realized in those early years that I was not in a *dysfunctional* family, but rather an *unappreciated* family. We were children who were just there. In my mind, we existed to be kept clean, fed, educated, and then off on our own as soon as possible. Enjoyment and good times rarely happened.

Life as a child in my family was just *okay*. It was not *wonderful*, and I *wanted* wonderful. I imagined that someday, when I was a parent, it *would* be wonderful. Bells and whistles would be going off. I would have fun and appreciate my children. What a concept!

Fast forward to 1993. It was my and my first husband Jim's twenty-fifth wedding anniversary. Our two adult daughters, Sharri and Amy, had thrown us a backyard party. Many of our original wedding party were there. Even our parish priest had come to officiate our exchange of renewal vows. The party was elegant, comfortable, and most definitely fun! We had lived in the same little tract house in a suburb of Los Angeles for twenty-four years. Our friends and neighbors were one. At one point, everyone participated in a conga line around the house. Toward the end of the evening, the DJ played "The Time of My Life," by Bill Medley. Everyone circled around us while we did our special variation of the two-step. Wow! As the party progressed, friends of our adult "kids" kept telling us how my husband and I had parented all of them in some way. Life doesn't get any better.

Parenting with Passion

We had our first daughter, Sharri, when I was twenty-one. She was terrific. She had the most beautiful blue eyes. As a new mommy, I loved and somewhat struggled through the baby time. It's an overwhelming job. I was able to stay home, even though we did not have much money. We made do with what we had, and life was good.

Then the toddler years came. My adorable baby daughter seemed to have grown fangs overnight. She talked. She walked. And she needed to be potty trained. One day, when the potty training was not going well, I snapped and spanked her. She looked at me as if I had put a dagger in her little heart. She was saying with her big blue eyes, "I'm doing the best I can." Nobody taught me how to potty train my child. Where was the manual? Where were the instructions?

The next day I was watching the *Today* show on television. Dr. Haim Ginott, a regularly featured guest, was talking about how we should not scold a child for what they cannot control. "For example," he said, "if your child trips, say, 'Oh, did that table get in your way?' It's better," he explained, "to blame an inanimate object because it doesn't have feelings."

Dr. Ginott made a lot of sense to me, so I bought his book, *Between Parent and Child*. Thirty years later, I still have that book close by my computer, where I now write. I have read it many times and attribute the birth of my passion for child development to this book.

Soon after reading it, my little Sharri and I were having a battle over picking up toys. She looked at me defiantly and said, "I hate you!" I calmly responded, "That's okay, because being a mommy is not a popularity contest." In other words, I was telling her that love has no boundaries. She was allowed to have her feelings. My guidance was her focus. Somehow, at that very instant, both Sharri and I knew that I was going to get through this parenting thing.

Eventually, my little toddler became a preschooler. At Sharri's school, moms were expected to help once a month. I'll never forget the first time Sharri and I sat at group time and watched the teacher sing, "Five little monkeys jumping on the bed." How cute, I thought. The art and activities were wonderful. As soon as I could, I enrolled in college classes to become a preschool teacher. The study of child development was just emerging. Working with children was hard, but rewarding. The welfare of my children and all of the children I could serve, has been my passion ever since. Yes, you can imagine wonderful parenting, and it can become real.

Your Own Childhood Family Sculpture

With some crayons or felt-tip pens, on a plain piece of paper, draw a picture of your childhood family. Place the members of your family of origin close to each other or far away, depending on where each person was in relation to the others. For example, if your mom and dad were close, place them next to each other. If they were divorced, place them farther apart. Place yourself and each sibling as close to or far away as your relationships were. Persons can be represented as simple circles, stick people, or more detailed, if desired. When you have finished drawing, color each person using your own color code. You may color your dad red because he was dynamic, your mom yellow because she was quiet, and so on. The colors you choose are totally up to you. You can use more than one color per person as long as it makes sense to your color-coding system. Next, explain your family sculpture drawing to your parenting partner or, for single parents, to a trusted friend. Have this person make one to share with you, also.

I've had students write volumes on each family member and sometimes submit this assignment in tears. Many times I have needed a box of tissues for myself while reading these reports. This exercise can bring up deep issues of abuse where professional counseling is needed. In most cases, these deeper emotions stay below the surface. The fear in us holds secrets like a sheet over our spirits. However, this act of releasing is just another step in making us stronger. Finally, many of the essays I have received are about support, love, and respect for their families. Reflecting upon your gifted experiences is well worth the time to boost your sense of purpose. Your wonderful heritage should encourage you to be the best you can be.

Forgiveness and Gratitude

When you look back on how you were parented as a child, some of you may need to embrace forgiveness. Your parents did the best they could at the time. Holding resentment for what you did not have as a child is pointless. A good method I learned from Dr. John Grey to release anger from past experiences is to write a letter to the person responsible for your anger, explaining how you feel. Do not send the letter. Then write a reply letter as if you were that person saying how sorry you are. Finally, write a third letter saying you forgive that person.

Do not rush this process. It may take days or even weeks to complete all three letters. It will help if you read these letters to a trusted friend. This exercise is so important because when you practice forgiveness, you get your future back in a whole new way.

I do not believe that all adults had unhappy childhoods. Many people have great parents and grandparents. Their task would be to write sincere thank-you letters to their parents and grandparents. If these people are still alive, send the letters to them. If they are no longer living, read your letters to a trusted friend. Expressing gratitude is a wonderful thing.

REFLECTIVE EXERCISE

Close your eyes and take a deep breath. Visualize the persons you need to forgive or give gratitude to in a loving way. Think of yourselves as communicating spirit to spirit. Know that your pain or joy is understood perfectly in this time together. Be grateful that you have this opportunity to experience each other in this special way.

Chapter Activities

In your workbook you will find the following activities:

- Family sculpture from your childhood
- Letters of forgiveness or gratitude

Congratulations! These are the first steps on your road to parenting from your spirit.

In the next chapter, you will learn how to choose the appropriate parenting style for yourself.

Most of us take parenthood seriously;
in a very real sense, we "go for broke" . . .
And then reality thuds against our plans.
What looked so simple turns out to be
far more complex.[1]
~ *Dorothy Corkille Briggs*

Finding the Spirit Within

Know my dear one,
    your life is but a path.
As your spirit joined us here on planet earth,
    you said, "I just want a good life. It is my birthright."
As you grew, you said,
    "Do I have to work this hard to get it?"
You asked, "Where are the parents who are strong like two
giant trees?
    Where is the plan to parent me with balance?
    Where is the healthy food to make my body strong?"
As you went to school, you said, "Where are the teachers that
love to teach?
    Where is the music, art, and plays?
    Where is the mirror to find myself?"
As you searched for a path to follow, you said,
    "Where is my passion?
    Which way should I go?
    Where is the focus?
    Where is the Light that knows?"
And after many tries and mistakes, learning one lesson after
    another, you looked one day and saw your path so clearly
    before you.
The Light is the Spirit that you brought with you
    here to planet earth.
You had it all along.
In your path through life, in your search for the Light,
    you have found yourself,
    your wonderful, beautiful, spiritual self.

~D. H. Summers

CHAPTER 2

Parenting Styles

Staying Out Late Exercise

Imagine that you are fifteen years old. Pretend that you are going to an athletic event at your high school, such as a football or basketball game, on a Friday night with your friends. You understand that you are expected home by 11:00 p.m. You end up coming home at 1:00 a.m.

- Are you *ignored*? Perhaps your parents are asleep or not at home and unaware that you got home so late. (1st Quadrant—Neglectful)

- Are your parents waiting up, wanting to discuss why you are late? Do they *listen to you* and believe your story? (2nd Quadrant—Democratic)

- Are your parents waiting up, upset because they are so worried about you? Then when they stop yelling, they hug you? (3rd Quadrant—Protective)

- Are your parents firmly waiting up, with a mix of anger and disappointment, ready to *ground* you? The determined time is extreme and firm. (4th Quadrant—Authoritative)

Share this possible episode with your parent partner or a trusted friend.

As an undergraduate student at California State University at Fullerton, I learned about these four basic parenting styles from Dr. Robert McLaren. In teaching child development over the years, I have used this knowledge as my foundation for explaining how parents raise their children.

The Parenting Quadrants

Figure 1 (pages 16 and 17) illustrates the quadrants of separate parenting styles. It shows the intersection of two basic parental guidelines, control and attachment, each with a scale from high to low.

Basically, functional families fall close to center in these quadrants. Dysfunctional families fall anywhere in the outer areas.

Visualizing parenting this way makes us aware of the baggage that parents bring to their adult families. Some people repeat the parenting style they experienced as children. Others may swing to the opposite parenting style. Stress occurs when parents are in opposite quadrants.

Challenge yourself to "look outside the box" of your own quadrants to understand the possibilities you have.

Quadrant 1: Neglected Children

In the first quadrant, children are often ignored due to parents' busy modern lives. My guess is that an abundance of children are in this situation. Instead of "time out," these parents need to practice "time in." As crazy as it sounds, I would suggest including family time in  appointment books and personal calendars, just like any other appointment. Actually, organized parent/child activities on a regularly scheduled evening can really work. An organization called Indian Guides and Indian Princesses has special outings arranged on a regular basis. Look to church, school, and other community groups to join for special organized events.

Also in this quadrant are parents who are present physically but not emotionally. Often this is due to various vices, such as alcoholism or drug abuse. Some neglectful parents are unaware that obsessive behaviors like constant work, overeating, or indulgent sexual practices can affect the quality of their parenting. A significant event usually needs to happen, like a death, arrest, job loss, or a severe illness before they can see the problem. For persons like this, John Bradshaw points to the importance of "surrendering" to treatment and a healing process.[2] Persons who participate in twelve-step programs know how well they work, and countless other self-help programs are available. Parents who focus on inappropriate behavior need to work through the pain of change.

Childhood passes so quickly. For many, there is no time to lose. Often, parental neglect can lead children of all economic levels to negative group experiences that support crime and illegal drug use.

Finally, one of the most difficult family crises is divorce. Both custodial and noncustodial parents need to communicate and to honor visiting times. There is nothing sadder than a child waiting for a parent who does not show up. It's even harder when one parent moves so far away that frequent visiting is impossible.

Ultimately, behavior problems in neglected children have a tendency to "run amuck" due to inconsistency. Busy parents and those who share caregiving with them need to work together so that children know where they stand. People in caregiving professions, teachers, grandparents, and neighbors with some extra time can help neglected children tremendously. A positive comment, noticing a talent and supporting it, a hug, or just taking the time to listen can really help to sustain these children. Many of them survive because of the supportive care they receive from

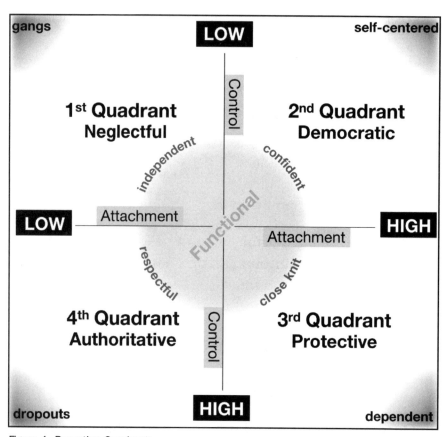

Figure 1. Parenting Quadrants

Parenting Outside the Box

1st Quadrant Control and Attachment are low.

Parents:	Neglect their children
Inner circle:	Children fend for themselves and learn to be *independent*
Outer circle:	Children can turn toward peers or *gangs* for acceptance

2nd Quadrant   **Control is low and Attachment is high.**

Parents:	Provide democracy through choice
Inner circle:	Children are *confident* and creative
Outer circle:	Children become overbearing, running the family, and can become *self-centered*

3rd Quadrant   **Attachment and Control are high.**

Parents:	Surround their children with love and concern for their well-being
Inner circle:	Children and parents are *close-knit* and always there for each other
Outer circle:	Children become overwhelmed, unable to make decisions on their own and can become *dependent*

4th Quadrant   **Control is high and Attachment is low.**

Parents:	Control by being strict
Inner circle:	Children know where they stand, are respectful, and have good citizenship
Outer circle:	Children are burdened by their parents

"back-up" parents in the community. This help often gives them a boost to become *independent* and focused on taking care of not only themselves but also others.

Quadrant 2: Democratic Children

The second quadrant represents parents who really want children and who are secure in letting them be self-thinkers. Here is where Dr. Haim Ginott excelled. He believed that behavior limits should exist only as needed, and consequences should be given only when necessary. He believed in a process of listening and evaluating in every situation. The downside of this style is that parents can be so understanding or *permissive* that their children take advantage of them by being self-centered. The line between parent and child must always exist. Ginott stated, "The parent must like his children, but he must not have an urgent need to be liked by them every minute of the day."[3]

Parents in this quadrant allow their children to choose the elective classes and extra activities they want to do. They support what their *children* love to do, not what *they* want them to do. Democratic parents communicate for discipline. This parenting style uses basic positive discipline with praise for good deeds. Tangible rewards like money or gifts are not part of this system.

This quadrant also includes the *era of focus*. After high school, it can take years for young people to find their purpose. Parents in the democratic quadrant help their children to find their passion in life. Doing this takes exceptional effort and patience. In the extreme, democratic parenting may very well exhaust even the most positive of parents, but the effort is well worth it. These children become *confident*, take risks, use their imagination, and create wonderful things.

Quadrant 3: Protected Children

The third quadrant shows the protective style of parenting. Some parents have asked me, "But isn't it important to protect your children in this day and age?" Of course it is important to make sure your children are safe and not in harm's way. This quadrant has its good and bad points, just as the other quadrants do. Children of protective parents will feel loved and the center of attention. Parents who are protective really want their children and love them more than life itself, but in that process may tend to smother or overprotect them. As youngsters, these children are never out of sight of either parent or someone extremely trusted like a grandparent. They are often kept from discovery, risks of any type, and the opportunity and joy of playing with other children. As they grow up, their interests do not emerge. They cannot get excited about certain things because they have not had the opportunity to experience the world.

In extreme cases where children are overprotected, they become *dependent*. They can be passionless and, therefore, raised without purpose. As they grow, school becomes drudgery. They may not even finish high school and turn to drugs or teenage pregnancies due to the overwhelming feelings they have. Often, parents who overprotect their children end up raising their grandchildren because their adult children are incapable. This is a very sad situation.

If you tend to fall into this quadrant, try to let go by allowing your children to go to birthday parties without you. Have your children join organizations like Girl Scouts or Boy Scouts. Let them go on overnight trips to friends' homes with parents you trust. Allow them to walk home from school with a friend. I know it will be hard, but children need a certain degree of freedom to grow, just like a plant needs water and light. Also, it helps to take interest in something you like yourself. Diverting your focus even a little will allow your child the space she needs to grow. However, when these parents are balanced, the benefit is a *close knit family*. Members are there for each other, creating a positive, loving experience.

Quadrant 4: Authoritative Children

In the fourth quadrant, authoritative parents are very clear about rules and consequences that will prevail. Researcher Dianna Baumrind supports this method as being the best way to raise children.[4] It is very clear in these households what the rules are and what punishments will be enacted if the rules are broken. Tangible rewards, like money for good grades or special outings are common with authoritative parenting. Expectations are always clear, such as behavioral standards or the profession the parents feel would be best for the child. Often, parents will choose activities, and their children will listen and usually respect what the parents have asked of them. Even when objections are raised, parents usually have the last word. In time, children who are raised in this manner seem to fare well in their education. They take the proper exams to enter college, apply with their parents' help, and attend college usually with good grades. However, they can be *passionless*. Sometimes they graduate from college and get a job, but they don't love it. Sometimes, they rebel—stand up for themselves, or choose a path they really want. Their parents may hyperventilate, but they usually concede. Consensus occurs when these parents see their children as successful, happy adults.

In the extreme, this style turns into an authoritarian approach. Parents who pursue this style are usually very disciplined themselves. They encounter problems when they focus on their goals for their children with so much control that the children rebel early in life. For example, a child who is not allowed to go on a family weekend event because a math score was not to the parents' expectation may harbor so much anger that he reacts by failing the course altogether. Some of these children are under so much pressure to fulfill their parents' expectations that they cheat on school assignments to avoid the wrath of their parents. These parents need to recognize the stress they impose on their children and let up. Again, leaning toward the center is always best.

When authoritative parenting is done right, children become *respectful*. They develop leadership qualities to benefit the whole community.

Just for Fun, Let's Add Mnemonics

Figure 2 illustrates the use of using a mnemonic word association for each of the quadrants. The neglected children need to fend for themselves; they may often act as if they are in control, so I call them the *Cool Cats*. The democratic children have it pretty easy with loving parents always being positive, so I call them the *Lucky Ducks*. The protected children do not have a lot of choices in life, so I like to think of them as the *Scared Kittens*. Then the last group are often pushed so much that they may look great on the outside but may have insecurities on the inside. I like to think of them as beautiful *Show Dogs*.

Figure 2. Quadrant Word Association

Evaluating the Quadrants

The quadrants help us to see how each of us was raised, as well as how our partners were raised. Parents need to "look outside their box" to evaluate their own childhoods and recognize the unique experience they had. Difficult experiences can build character. Wonderful experiences can provide enrichment. Use the quadrants as a check to balance your emotional baggage. Look at both the good and the bad stuff, and realize that you can choose how to parent your children.

In my classroom teaching, I use the film *Parenthood*, starring Steve Martin and directed by Ron Howard, to illustrate the parenting quadrants. I suggest you rent the film and observe the different quadrants as they emerge. The humor and drama of this film deliver many points that you will relate to in one way or another.

Then review Figure 1, Parenting Quadrants, on pages 16 and 17. Go out to dinner with your spouse (for single parents, do this activity on your own or with a close friend) and discuss how you were parented and how you want to parent using the basic intersection of two lines. I like to picture parents using paper napkins at a restaurant to do this. Analyze all of it. Rather than argue about how to raise your children, build respect for your differences, honor your individual styles, and work as a team toward balance. It would be great if engaged couples would evaluate this concept before they even think about having children.

Mending Our Troubled Spirits

Consider the following message from Robert Fulghum concerning the grandfather he never knew:

> In a sense we make up all our relatives, though. Fathers, mothers, brothers, sisters and the rest, especially if they are dead or distant. We take what we know, which isn't ever the whole story, and we add it to what we wish and need, and stitch it together into some kind of family quilt to wrap up in on our mental couch.

We even make ourselves up, fusing what we are with what we wish into what we must become. I'm not sure why it must be so, but it is. It helps to know this. Thinking about the grandfather I wish I had prepares me for the grandfather I wish to be, a way of using what I am to shape the best that is to come. It is a preparation.

Sometime, not too far from now, a child will call out "Grandfather" and I will know what to do.[5]

Reading this quote can help you think about how much you can mend your troubled spirits from the disappointments of your childhood. If your parents were lacking in a particular quality, embrace that quality and be the wonderful mom or dad you wish you had had as a child. By doing this, you can be healed.

Focusing on the Best Way to Raise Children

Any of the four parenting styles is *functional* as long as you are centered. Balancing control and attachment is the essential factor. Follow these centering rules:

1. For Quadrant 1, busy *neglectful* parents, set aside time to be with your children

2. For Quadrant 2, indulgent *democratic* parents, be clear about your house rules and be firm with consequences

3. For Quadrant 3, careful *protective* parents, lighten up by trusting your children with some freedom and allowing them to make decisions

4. For Quadrant 4, strong *authoritative* parents, allow your children to make choices within your own boundaries and ease up on the small stuff

Most important, realize that the possibilities within the quadrants are infinite. Each child is raised differently. Firstborn children have *experimental* first-time parents. Younger children in the family have *experienced* parents. The focus is different for boys and for girls. Children's needs vary depending on their physical and mental capabilities. Opportunities will deviate due to social and economic status. Finally, situations will fluctuate depending on the prevailing consciousness of the community.

I perceive the possibilities of the quadrants like stars in the night. The next time you observe a clear night sky full of stars, imagine each of us as a child of the universe. Imagine each of us as a light, here on planet Earth to find our passion and fulfill our purpose in life. As parents, you are your children's first teachers. Honor the light. Help them find their passion. Support the fulfillment of  their purpose. Open to your support systems. Know the magnificence of your child as he emerges. The real prize for doing a good job of parenting is that you will also witness your own magnificence.

REFLECTIVE EXERCISE

Close your eyes and take a deep breath. Visualize working together to achieve the perfect parenting style. Know that you are able to do this in a loving, positive way. Be grateful that you will be able to bring balance and harmony into your family.

Chapter Activities

In your workbook you will find the following activities:

- *Parenthood* video review
- Your own Parent Quadrant realization
- Open letter to your children

After you have written your letter, move on to the next chapter to find your perfect parenting partner.

Love and marriage, love and marriage,
Go together like a horse and carriage.
This I tell you, brother,
You can't have one, you can't have one,
You can't have one without the other.
~ *Rogers and Hammerstein*[1]

Finding Your Soul Mate

Loving means to love yourself first.
It is knowing that all of the things you want in a mate are
already the attributes of you.

The feeling when first you meet is a special space when
time stops, rockets go off, and the earth stops rotating.

Joy to those who are strong, independent souls that unite.
Blessed are those who breathe life, not take life from the
one they love.

Abundance to those who are bound in trust and have respect for
each other's goals and passions.

For breathing life into each other's spirit—as we are human, as we
are parents, as we are partners—is the ultimate experience.

~D. H. Summers

CHAPTER 3

Parenting Partners

Happiness in Marriage

New relationships start with honeymoon periods. All is wonderful, new, and exciting. Figure 3 illustrates the levels of happiness in a marriage for couples raising children. In the early years of parenting, things are fairly simple. Yes, the hours are long; but, for the most part, joy overcomes fatigue. For moms and dads, parenting challenges really do not emerge until the preteen years, when hormones and independence enter the family structure. The most stressful parenting time is often the post-high-school era, or

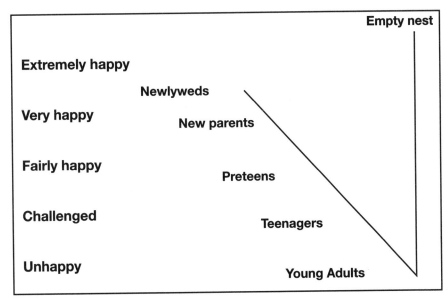

Figure 3. Happiness in Marriage

what I call the time of the *focus* mantra. Focus! Focus! Focus! Pick something! For many young adults, choosing a career path and getting the proper training can be a ruthless task. Basically, from the time the oldest child reaches twelve until the youngest is on her own, the struggle of parenting magnifies. Simply stated, the parenting style you start in infancy can set the stage for twenty to thirty years of your life, depending on how many children you have. Good parenting styles pay off in the end, mostly with *relief.* Raising good, healthy children is the *biggest* job you will ever do. So I say, pick your parenting partner carefully. When couples are compatible, trust each other, and communicate, raising children is much easier.

Opposites Attract but May Not Make the Best Mates

When I married my first husband, our attraction was strong. We were in our late teens and enjoyed all the romance and joy that many young couples feel. However, when it came to parenting, we were not on the same page. I had been in the *Neglectful* quadrant, and he had been parented in the *Democratic* quadrant. My intense desire to be the perfect parent led to years of study, communication, and some difficult experiences. We worked many issues into the ground and came up with as much balance as we could manage. Thank God! At times, when things were most difficult, we learned that we just had to *work it out.*

What does "work it out" mean? For us, *working it out* turned out to be learning to trust each other. We went to a Marriage Encounter program one weekend with our church. We learned to listen and express ourselves on a *feeling* level. You could describe us as small sapling trees. We were only twenty and twenty-one years old when we got married. Strong marriages require that each person be a big strong tree. We both needed to be individuals and not *dependent* on each other. We realized that the real key to survival was to give each other and ourselves space to follow our passions and to grow into our full adult potential. Allowing that strength to emerge gave us the opportunity to trust. Within that bond of trust, we found the *power to parent*. If you cannot find a Marriage Encounter program in your community, ask around at different churches or counseling services for something similar.

Face it. Relationships are hard work, but without them we would not get the rewards they can bring. I like what Dr. Barbara De Angelis says about relationships:

> Relationships are an instant and continual training ground. They insist that you look in the mirror at yourself; they reveal all the parts of you that are not loving. They show you your dark side. They knock on the door of your heart, demanding that you open the places you've kept locked. And then, every day and night, they give you an opportunity to practice love, to stretch yourself beyond what is comfortable, and to keep doing it better.[2]

List All You Want in a Mate

After my first husband died, I wanted another person in my life. I found help from a very wise woman, Dr. Edith Edger, who told me to make a list of everything I wanted in a new mate. After I made my list, she said in a hushed tone, "Be all those things, and you will attract that perfect person." My list had seventeen items on it. Several months later, I met a wonderful man who possessed all seventeen qualities. Amazing, but true! Two years later, he became my second husband. Now we have, between us, seven wonderful grandchildren and a truly great life together. So, those of you who are looking for that perfect partner, start making your list and embrace the qualities on that list.

Wouldn't it be great if we were all totally mature adults when we found the person we wanted to marry? Consider how nice it would be if we could have our second or even third relationship first, after learning about ourselves and what we want. Many of you are in your first marriage with children and facing the challenges it brings. It is too late to make that all-you-want list, so now you have to face the realization that you cannot change your mate to fit your idea of perfection. It is important that you not try to change your partner into something that you desire to *make yourself happy*. If you are not happy, the only thing you can change is yourself in some way. And guess what? That *thing* you need to change may be *acceptance*.

Here is an example of acceptance. My first husband was very critical of many things, especially of what I would say or do around other people. As soon as we would get into the car after a social event, he would have a list of what I should not have said or done. One day it occurred to me that this was *his* challenge—his desire to be perfect. It was his, not mine. I decided at that moment that I would not allow *his* concern for perfection to upset or bother me. This was a huge step for me. From then on, I accepted that this was just the way he was and I never let it bother me again.

Instead of getting upset with a headache or digestive problem, I just let him be the person he needed to be. However, practicing acceptance of others does not mean that you should be a doormat. If everything else is good in your relationship, you may just need to accept some things you cannot change.

Acceptance works both ways. Your partner needs to accept certain things he or she cannot change about you. Think this through. How would *you* like to be married to *you*? Yes, love has its challenges!

Trial Marriages

I am a member of the baby-boomer generation. In the 1960s and 1970s, we had a reputation for being protesters and wanting to change social norms. Most of us married young, had children, and settled into typical mainstream America. One outstanding feature of our generation has been our divorce rate—fifty percent!

Now our children have decided to one-up us with *trial marriages*—living together. As one of my college students put it, "In our generation, we're expected to live together for about a year and then be engaged for a year before we get married." Okay, how are we, as parents, to handle this? As my oldest daughter told me in her "living together" phase, "Mom, you know we just might have the right idea here."

Some people say that living together does not produce fewer divorces. I say time will tell. I think it will take several decades to see the true results. Nonetheless, the die is cast. It seems like everyone is doing it. Even the most conservative churches marry "live-ins." Sometimes marriages start with one or more children already. In some cases, the children are even in the wedding party or symbolically part of the ceremony itself. Trial marriages are with us for better or for worse. My guess is that it's for the better. What do you think?

Stepmoms

I once went to a lecture that had a very interesting title, "Step Moms." Since I was about to marry my second husband and technically become a *stepmom*, I decided to go. Two attractive ladies told their story; one was the "real" mom and the other was the stepmom. They talked about how they played these awful, nasty lifestyle antics with each other. Greetings on the phone were very strained. Whenever they were both in the same room, it was like two icebergs clashing. Parent conferences were a real mockery of the interested parents they both were. The ten-year-old boy they were both parenting was becoming a victim of their hurt, fearful spirits. Then one day all hell broke loose! They got into a huge fight over shoes. One had the same shoes on as the other one. Go figure! Well, they got into it. Then, for some reason they began laughing. They finally decided to work together with a family counselor. The end result is a book called *Step Moms* and a website, *www.stepmoms.com*.

I think these two women are terrific. I expect to see them on *Oprah* someday. The bottom line with this story is that they discovered they had to replace their feelings of anger and hurt with feelings of love. The child for whom they shared parenting responsibilities needed love from both his "real" mom and his stepmom. Approaching the other parent or parents of the children you all are raising with love in your heart will pay off in the end. Children expect love. They especially need love when the family has been uprooted by a divorce to make them feel secure.

I challenge you divorced parents and stepparents to respect all your parenting partners, including former spouses. Forgive the issues you have with them for the sake of both your children and yourselves. You may want to go back to the forgiveness exercises in Chapter 1 and work at forgiveness every day. You will know that you are healed when you realize the gift you learned from the pain you endured. It is hard to believe, but when the day comes that you realize what you learned—whether it is more patience, a better appreciation for life, or whatever—you will know why it happened and experience the bliss of resolution.

Single Parents

Single parents make up a large portion of the parents in America. A prominent reason is the agonizing excess baggage that adults bring to their relationships. Drs. Lewis and Marge Rosenblat from Durango, Colorado, have done some interesting work documenting the challenges of single parents. Their theory is that divorce is often a relief. The weakest parent often succumbs to some abusive state, such as alcoholism, drugs, gambling, codependency, or constant focus on career. The surviving single parent then takes on a stronger role based on sheer will and determination. A benefit these single parents gain is developing a sense of autonomy. The Rosenblats also discovered that the children of single parents do just fine. Drawings that the children have made of their families, have demonstrated contentment with the single-parent families that they have. With only one parent, childhood becomes a different adventure. Support of extended family and community can help.[3] Overall, life teaches them to be self-reliant. I believe that determination, which comes from surviving different experiences, can produce motivated, dynamic persons who add much to society.

Finding a sense of one's spirit can be a long and hard journey. Sometimes it takes a failed relationship for us to step up to the plate. The salient aspect is distress, but there is light at the end of the tunnel. New opportunities, like a better mate or passion for your work, often come along to soothe your troubled heart.

Support and Love in Marriage

Two of the biggest issues that couples fight over are money and raising their children. For both issues, communication and trust are essential. Respect for each other's adult career paths is helpful, too. If one of you wants to go to college, open a business, or move to a new location, it's important for the other partner to back up this dream. There is nothing worse than suppressing someone's passion out of fear. Be happy that your loved one has dreams and passion for life. Isn't that why you fell in love in the first place?

More than anything, parents need a strong sense of loving each other. They need to have time away from the children. Just because you are married, don't forget to date. Dinner and a movie can help reduce stress in a relationship. Also, at least once a year, go away for a weekend. This is especially important to do for your anniversary. Focus on just the two of you. Discover where you are now. Make plans for your future. Commit to supporting each other's spiritual growth. The parent bond needs to be strong to sustain the *balance* you need to raise children. So, parents, take time to love your parent partner. You both deserve it.

Close your eyes and take a deep breath. Visualize your perfect marriage. Whatever you both like doing, see yourselves doing it. Know that as you are doing wonderful things together, you can also have great communication to be the perfect partners. Also know that you can support each other through trust to be the perfect parents you want to be. Be thankful and happy knowing that you are able to be together in this life.

Chapter Activities

In your workbook you will find the following activities:

- List the qualities you desire in a partner
- List the qualities you wish your partner would have
- List all the favorite things you like to do as a couple

In the next chapter, you will learn how to handle the various stages of your life.

The meaning of life is to love and to work.

~ *Sigmund Freud*[1]

A Kid

A kid, any kid, needs to know he'll be picked up when he falls.

A kid, any kid, needs choices like, "Hey, Dude, what shirt do you want to wear today?"

A kid, any kid, needs time to play with friends, paint with her fingers, and blow bubbles all day.

A kid, any kid, needs to go on outings to the park, beach, or zoo.

A kid, any kid, needs grandparents to adore her when she performs at her recitals and sporting events.

A kid, any kid, needs to be taught to read, write, do math, play an instrument, dance, and sing.

A kid, any kid, deserves it all: trust, choices, freedom to initiate, the chance to learn and find passion for life.

A kid, any kid, needs you to be a parent who provides it all with your time, energy, joy, and love.

~D. H. Summers

CHAPTER 4

Life Stages

The Stages of Your Life

Erik Erikson has always fascinated me. Whether you have heard of this great thinker of the twentieth century or not, you will undoubtedly be affected by his profound discussion of the life cycle. The essence of his work shows how life can play itself out perfectly. Erikson theorized that people live life successfully or not as a result of both psychological and sociological reasons. His highly meaningful work will help you see where you have been, where you are now, and where your future is headed.

Erikson studied under Ana Freud (Sigmund's daughter) and Maria Montessori before he became a professor at Harvard early in the twentieth century. At one point, he took a sabbatical to explore the indigenous cultures of North America. He lived with several different Native American tribes for a year. His experience, along with his extraordinary insight, taught him how passing through life's stages is significant in providing fulfillment. His science-oriented spiritual understanding of life is genuine and truly perceptive.[2]

Erikson Evaluated

Erikson saw that the indigenous North American people intently served the basic needs of their infants. This led to trust, the essential element of all social structures. As toddlers, children were given choices. Soon they showed initiative in what they wanted to do. Eventually, they learned skills from their elders in things they were interested in. This led to having identity within the group. After learning their skills and achieving success, they were able to choose a mate. Because of pride in their identities, they possessed intimacy within their marriages. As parents, they taught their children, passing on their knowledge to the next generation. By the time they became grandparents, they had achieved a fulfilled life. Later in his life, Erikson summarized each of the eight life stages in one word: [3]

Between Ages

Between	Ages	
0 – 2	When babies have basic *trust*, they have	*Hope*
3 – 5	When preschool children have *autonomy*, they have	*Will*
5 – 11	When school-age children have *initiative*, they have	*Purpose*
11 – 18	When teenagers have *industry*, they have	*Competence*
18 – 25	When young adults have *identity*, they have	*Fidelity*
25 – 40	When adults have *intimacy*, they have	*Love*
40 – 70	When mature adults pass on knowledge to the next *generation*, they show	*Care*
70 – Death	When senior adults have *integrity*, they show	*Wisdom*

What does this mean for parents of the twenty-first century?

To understand Erikson's theory better, answer the questions in your Chapter 4 activities.

Quadrant 1: Neglectful Parents

Parents need to realize the importance of fulfilling their child's basic needs. So when you are home, be as attentive as possible. When you cannot be with your child, make sure your caregiver is keeping your child not only clean and fed, but also rocked and held with love.

Sometimes even moms who are home get their priorities mixed up. One of my favorite authors, Dr. Virginia Axline, tells about an exceptional case study. A very intelligent preschool child was considered retarded due to his parents' lack of attachment. His mother frequently locked him in his room because she considered him the reason why she could not work or be respected as a doctor anymore. Dibs, the preschool child, was unwilling to socialize with other children at his preschool. Eventually, after working with Dibs, Dr. Axline achieved success with him through loving play therapy and interaction with the mother. He went on to become a very comfortable social child full of hope, will, purpose, and competence.[4] Unfortunately, not every neglected child gets this special treatment.

Stress from various sources seems to overwhelm even the best of parents. Look to extended family and the community for support. Children can get their basic needs fulfilled from many sources. Just make sure the source is wholesome, and your children will be fine.

Quadrant 2: Democratic Parents

Democratic parents often deal with overload. In their quest to offer lots of choices and attachment, they involve their children in too many activities. This can be draining. Parents need to provide their children with downtime—time to reflect and absorb the serenity of life.

The main pitfall for democratic parents is that they produce pockets of neglect. Sometimes they neglect one of their children; sometimes they neglect their adult relationship. Dr. Salvador Menuchin had an interesting case study. A family with five children had a near-death experience with their fourth child. She had become severely anorexic. With family therapy, Dr. Menuchin determined that the fourth child refused to eat because it was the only way for her to get the attention of the family. So, for the sake of everyone, he suggested that they all slow down. He also suggested that the mother and father work on their intimacy, which they had been neglecting. Doing these things helped the whole family[5]. So, parents, stop running "amuck." Get a sitter and go out to dinner. Better yet, take a weekend vacation. Occasional alone time is essential for a strong, trusting bond. The whole family will be better off. Remember, without your *love*, your family wouldn't exist in the first place.

Quadrant 3: Protective Parents

Protective parents should first learn to trust themselves. Often parents in this quadrant are stuck in a place where they cannot achieve what they want in life. Circumstances, like an early pregnancy, may have kept them from obtaining the skills they need for a better job. They may need to go to continuation high school or college. If you are in this situation, you may be afraid to make choices because of the mistrust you have experienced in life. Maybe a good support group of encouraging, positive friends will help to give you confidence. Take the time to go beyond the protective fence you have built around yourself. Volunteer for an activity. Perhaps in that environment you will find an interest. Allow yourself to have your dreams. Allow yourself the freedom to fly, and your children will fly as well.

The Head Start program in the United States has always focused on the parents' sense of achievement as well as the youngsters'. Longitudinal studies have proved that parents who have respect and dignity for themselves raise more positive children, who graduate from high school and go on to higher educations. Productive, healthy parents usually produce productive, healthy children.

Quadrant 4: Authoritative Parents

Authoritative parents need to offer choices. Allowing children to make *some* decisions is essential. Start with small choices for your toddler. "Do you want to wear this or that shirt today?" As they get older, they can choose the extra activities they want to do. Let them pick the elective classes they want to take in middle and high school. By accepting their choices, you give your child a sense of autonomy or independence. Ultimately, you do not want your children to feel guilty about failing your expectations. As they get older, they need to make big choices. Gary Zukav tells us, "Only through responsible choice can you choose consciously to cultivate and nourish the needs of your soul and to challenge and release the wants of your personality."[6] When you allow your children to make choices, you give them the gift of learning through their mistakes. Feeling the emotions of sadness and even rage can help your children to find things that they are passionate about. This passion may be the very element that gives them the purpose to accomplish awesome results. As loving parents, your heart may be in the right place to insist on this or that for your children. The bottom line is, however, that it is *their* lives they are living, *not yours*.

Your Life Cycle Plan

Erikson set a standard for social-emotional health with his eight-stage life cycle. His conclusions have given us an example to work with in the twenty-first century. Loving your *self* and your *children* will provide *productive spirits* for the universe.

REFLECTIVE EXERCISE

Close your eyes and take a deep breath. Visualize your children as adults. See them as happy and joyful. Know that because of your nurturing, they have found their perfect life professions and relationships filled with creativity and joy. Be grateful in your ability to give love so they have love in their lives.

Chapter Activities

In your workbook you will find the following activities:

- Questions on the Erikson Stages
- Plan to achieve success for yourself
- Plan to achieve success for your children

In the next chapter, we will explore disciplinary styles and techniques.

Parental discipline may eventually lead to self-discipline.
By identifying with the parents and the values they personify,
the child attains inner standards for self-regulation.
~*Dr. Haim Ginott*[1]

There Is a Day

As a parent, there is a day when . . .
You say something . . . and then, you say to yourself,
"Oh, my God, I sound just like my parent."
Don't feel bad.
It happens to everyone.

It's that moment when you really stop and think,
"Is what I am doing the right thing?
Did saying those things make me a better person?"
You can't help but squirm and wonder.
Then there is a little voice inside you that speaks and says . . .
"Be gentle, be loving, but be strong and give appropriate
guidance."

There is a little voice that also says, "You can do it."

~D. H. Summers

CHAPTER 5

Discipline

Three Different Temperaments

When my second daughter, Amy, was two years old, I took her to an outdoor swap meet. After shopping for awhile, she decided not to go any farther. She had a tantrum face down in the dirt. There was no talking her out of this one. The more I tried to get her up, the more she kicked and screamed. "Fine," I said, "I'll just leave you here." I walked a few yards and slipped behind a vendor's booth. I thought Amy would pick herself up and come running for Mommy, her source of abundance. No such luck. There she remained, kicking and screaming. For a second, I thought, Oh! Someone may take my darling Amy. Not a chance. Who in their right mind would take a screaming, kicking toddler? Then I felt my guardian angel guide me to love and accept Amy just the way she was. At that point I was able to pick her up and take her to the car.

At times like this, you really wonder why any of us want to be parents at all. However, we all know the benefits. Hugs and kisses make up for tantrums in the end. In their research on temperament, Thomas and Chess found the following four genetically pre-determined types in infants:[2]

Easy temperament	40 percent
Slow to warm up	15 percent
Difficult	10 percent
Combination	35 percent

Additional facts indicate that temperament trends remain

integrated in a youngster's personality. Overall, however, studies conclude that evolution over time allows for a variety of change. This is where *nurturing* or *parenting* prevails over *nature*, your genetic code. The enormous difference is how the child's personality matches with the parents'—commonly called *goodness of fit*. This is where discipline, which comes from the Latin word *discipulus* (meaning *to teach*), comes into play. Let us now examine how the parenting-style quadrants establish the *cause* and *effect* of children's personality development.

The Three-Ring Circus

Whenever I lecture on the parenting quadrants, I get approached at the break (even in the restroom) over this issue. Someone will say, "I am in the Democratic quadrant, but my spouse is in the Authoritative quadrant, and we are having the worst time raising our kids." I call this the Passive-Aggressive Syndrome. The result causes arguing. When arguing about the children escalates, the situation is reflected in an abyss of uncertainty. Anger creates fear, which forces children, who are in the middle, into survival mode. In order to climb out, youngsters will use one parent over the other. For example, they will get permission to go someplace from the *passive* parent (Neglectful or Democratic), not even considering asking the *aggressive* one (Authoritative or Protective). This causes a break in trust between the parents. A three-ring circus is the result, illustrated in Figure 4, also known as the Dysfunctional Rings of Chaos.

Are you living in a three-ring circus? If so, consider these five disciplinary rules:

1. Commit to trust each other

2. Support each other's decisions

3. Discuss issues in private

4. Agree to rules and limits

5. Be consistent

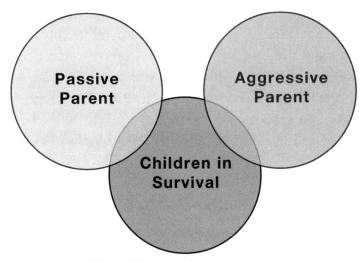

Figure 4. Dysfunctional Rings of Chaos

Positive versus Negative Spiral

In one of my parenting classes, a mother told me, "I give my kids three chances before giving a punishment." I asked her, "Do they do it three times?" "Yes," she said. "Well then," I responded, "You're setting yourself up for failure. Think about it. The behavior you do not want will have two more *chances* permitted by you."

I believe in working with a positive spiral. Communicate your expectations clearly. Say, "I expect you to do your homework." When the homework is done, give praise. Respond with, "Awesome. I knew you could do it." Perhaps your child has not done her homework. Work with trust by asking, "What's going on?" Perhaps there is a conflict of understanding the assignment. Maybe your child needs a good medical work-up. Perhaps your child is part of the 15 to 20 percent of children genetically predisposed to dyslexia and needs a special tutor. Whatever it is, we need to understand what's behind it. Our children need our assistance in coping with the rigors of learning the complex skills of life.

Some time ago, a couple told me that if their teenage son, an only child, did not have a B average or better by Thursday, he could not go snow skiing with them on Friday. I never found out if the son went skiing; but six months later, the parents told me how upset they were that he was not going to graduate from high school because of his bad grades and cutting school. They were so upset they packed his clothes and put them on the doorstep. Then they changed all the locks on the house and refused to let him in. "Let him see what life is like out there without our help," they said. Five years later, I ran into these parents and asked about their son. They told me he was a bouncer at a bar. Sadly, he had chosen a way to make money to survive, but not a path that would bring him fulfillment. Now in his thirties, he is taking some classes at a community college and trying to move forward with his life. Sometimes, the only control a child has is not to turn in homework or not to go to school. This is an example of united parents, but where were they headed? They were in a negative spiral.

The Quadrants and Discipline

Quadrant 1: Neglectful to Ignoring Parents

Discipline in this quadrant is inconsistent. Punishments are actually given, but usually without any follow-through. Rules and limits are unclear, if ever given. Family discussions are rare events.

When ignored, children reach for any parent they can get. The old movie *Stand By Me* shows how the resourcefulness of kids can prevail. In this story, two boys were abandoned. One had grief-stricken parents due to an accidental death of one of his siblings. The other child had a single alcoholic parent. In the course of several episodes in the summer when they both turned twelve, the boys learned to parent each other with acts of trust. This is a beautiful story. However, in real life, a stark outcome can occur. Children turning to other children for parenting can lead to gang companionship. This can happen in any neighborhood—inner-city children are not the only ones who fall into peer parenting. Suburban and rural children experience gang situations as well.

The lucky children in this quadrant find themselves in Boys or Girls Clubs, church youth organizations, and so on, where they learn to be independent young adults who are often focused on helping others.

Quadrant 2: Democratic to Permissive Parents

In a democratic parenting style, children rule. They make the choices. They learn to be convincing at all times to get the sympathy of their *understanding* parents.

The major pitfall for parents is becoming a doormat. In one of my parenting classes, the mother of a four-year-old boy told me that he was not potty-trained. I said, "Really? He is four!" The youngster overheard my comment and marched defiantly across the room. "I like my diapers and I'm going to keep them." Can you imagine what he is going to be like when he is fifteen years old? I don't want to be there. When you are a parent in this quadrant, you need to stand up for yourself. Say "No" and mean it. I believe that many parents who turn to a tough-love approach were permissive parents when their difficult child was in preschool. Be careful and be strong when you need to be. Remember never be a doormat for your kids. You are the parent—they are not.

Quadrant 3: Protective to Overprotective Parents

The children in this quadrant need safe choices so that they have enough comfortable space to take risks, yet still have the freedom to be *creative* and to do wonderful things.

The media frequently reports on tragedies involving children. There are abductions, abuse from strangers, accidents, and so on. Life is difficult and sometimes bad things happen. In today's information age, everything is magnified. Sometimes you wonder if you shouldn't move to some remote village in Montana so that things will be better, safer. Well, Montana has problems, too. There is no escaping fear. The issue that parents face today is how to feel safe and secure without smothering their children.

In my neighborhood in the suburbs of Los Angeles, where I lived for thirty years, there was a lovely couple in their forties who had two darling little girls. As the girls grew, the parents became fearful. As a result, the girls could not go to birthday parties unless their parents stayed the whole time. Their parents took them to and from school every day until they were seniors in high school. They never dated or had many friends. The parents died when the girls were in their late teens, and the girls were devastated. It was difficult for them to sell the house. It took years for them to develop and move on to their adult lives.

Without any sense of independence, the rigors of adult life cannot go smoothly. Children in this quadrant will take on things they can control, such as what they eat, when they have sex, and so on. Often they do not stray far from their parents, who smother them because they do not know any better. This can create a social condition called co-dependency. These families also have secrets. They hide their deep fears of insecurity, which does an injustice to their children.

Allow as much freedom as you can if you are in this quadrant. Trust as much as you can. By doing so, you will have that close-knit family you want and still leave a legacy that your children will appreciate.

Quadrant 4: Authoritative to Authoritarian Parents

Authoritative parents want their way. They can see the light at the end of the tunnel. They are sound, organized, successful people who want their children to be as perfect as they can be. These parents are big on tangible awards. They will give money, trips—whatever it takes for their children to get A's on their report cards. Extra activities usually involve competition and winning. Talk about *pressure.*

I once read about a famous actress and her authoritative father, who was also a well-known actor. He was determined that his lovely daughter would go to college and become a teacher. This is what he wanted, and there was no way for her to say no. On the day that she graduated, she handed her dad her diploma and said, "Okay, Daddy, now can I become an actress?" Her famous father gave in. This example comes from love, but sometimes children take on a tremendous guilt complex because they *cannot* or *do not want* to fulfill their parents' expectations. I really believe that when parents raise children in this way, the children will do whatever it takes to get the grades, to get the scholarship, to get the degree, and finally, to get the job. In the end, they are not happy. Too much coercion can lead to disappointment.

So, parents in this quadrant, listen. Your children's spirits will direct them in their perfect purpose. All you need to do is redirect, love, and support them. This is how you will earn a *respectful* atmosphere in your home.

Honoring Emotions to Understanding the Limbic System

When I was a child, my family moved frequently. When I was about eight, we moved to a small town. We did not know anybody. When I lamented about how sad I was to leave my friends in Chicago, my father said, "Oh just forget it. You will make new friends." This type of response was typical, and I remember shrugging off my feelings of sadness. Years later, when I was reading Dr. Ginott, I loved his message about recognizing a child's emotions:

> Emotions are part of our genetic heritage. Fish swim, birds fly, and people feel. Sometimes we are happy, sometimes we are not; but sometimes in our life we are sure to feel anger and fear, sadness and joy, greed and guilt, lust and scorn, delight and disgust. While we are not free to choose the emotions that arise in us,

we are free to choose how and when to express them, provided we know what they are. That is the crux of the problem. Many people have been educated out of knowing what their feelings are. When they hated, they were told it was only dislike. When they were afraid, they were told there was nothing to be afraid of. When they felt pain, they were advised to be brave and smile. Many of our popular songs tell us, "Pretend you are happy when you are not."

What is suggested in the place of this pretense? Truth. Emotional education can help children to *know what they feel*. It is more important for a child to know what he feels than why he feels it. When he knows clearly what his feelings are, he is less likely to feel "all messed-up" inside.[3]

Because of Dr. Ginott, I always tried my best to honor my children's feelings. I would say things like, "It's okay to be sad," or "Boy, I can see you are really mad," or "It's neat to see you enjoying this activity."

I used to cringe when I went to the grocery store and noticed an upset child crying because he wanted something and the mother responding with something like, "I already told you once. You cannot have it because we cannot afford it. You'd better stop crying or I'll give you something to cry about." Of course, this would make the child cry even more. Then a spanking might happen right there on the spot. Now everyone in the parking lot could hear this child cry. It almost seems funny, except to the child who did not get his feelings recognized.

When my children wanted something I could not afford, I would use what Dr. Ginott taught me by saying, "Wow, that is really neat! I would love to buy that for you right now, but we just cannot afford it today. What we really need are some apples. Come over here and help me pick out some really nice ones." I used to love the power it gave me when I honored my children's feelings. Thank you, Dr. Ginott.

When I was a preschool teacher, we sang a really cute song:

If you're happy and you know it, clap your hands. CLAP, CLAP
If you're happy and you know it, clap your hands. CLAP, CLAP
If you're happy and you know it,
then your smile will surely show it.
If you're happy and you know it, clap your hands. CLAP, CLAP

To honor children's feelings, I would add:

If you're sad and you want to, you can cry. BOO HOO
If you're sad and you want to, you can cry. BOO HOO
If you're sad and you want to,
then your face will surely show it.
If you're sad and you want to, you can cry. BOO HOO

I then added, "If you're mad and you want to, stomp your feet," and so on. The children would also add their own feelings and actions and we would have fun with it. Try it sometime when you are bathing your children or driving someplace in the car. This song sets accepting feelings in the mind for future experiences.

The consciousness of the 1970s was focused on feelings. Back then, my children were young and I was teaching preschool. The Viet Nam War was just ending, and people were in touch with how they were feeling about a myriad of things. It was around this time that Marlo Thomas published her Grammy award-winning album *Free to Be You and Me*. It featured a popular football player, Rosie Grier, singing, "It's all right to cry." Incredible!

Today, current brain research backs up what Dr. Ginott and Marlo Thomas were sharing with us thirty years ago. Dr. Carla Hannaford told us in 1995:

> Emotions meet in the intersection of body and mind. This is almost literally true since most emotional processing occurs in the limbic system, the area that

lies between the reptilian brain and the cerebral cortex. The limbic system has links with the neocortex allowing for emotional/cognitive processing. It also works in concert with the body to elicit the physical signs of emotions, like the flush of embarrassment and the smile of joy. Limbic system emotions also determine the release of neurotransmitters that either strengthen or weaken our immune system. [4]

This tells me that accepting children's emotions is more important than we thought. Not only does it make them feel accepted and happy, but it is instrumental in providing good health.

Corporal Punishment to Conflict Resolution

In the last section, I mentioned how it was not uncommon to see a child being spanked in the grocery store. Are any of you observing this today? Well, I have not seen a child being spanked in public for a long time. Things have changed since the 1970s, and one of them is the frequent use of corporal punishment. In the 1980s a new concept for child rearing came into vogue: the *time-out* method. Everyone thought this was great. I can remember demonstrating it to my high-school students as the new effective way to get children to behave. We could make a misbehaving child sit in some designated place for an allotted amount of time. Usually the time-out was one minute for each year of the child—two minutes for a two-year-old, three minutes for a three-year-old, and so on. Young parents today were most likely raised with this method. I am not saying it was a wrong approach. It certainly helped to keep many children from getting spanked, and it helped to relieve the stress of tense situations. However, professional childcare persons like myself started noticing that it was not working. Yes, sitting out a tense situation was good. Children were not being beaten up by overly emotional parents. But, what children were learning from a time-out is how *not to behave*. The new approach is to learn how to behave through compromise and trust.

In the early 1990s, Lois Roberts, a professor at UCLA Extension, told us we needed to look more deeply into discipline techniques. She saw time-out being done so much that children were overly exposed or habituated to it and not learning appropriate behavior. Many rallied around her mantra of "Time-out is out."[5]

About that time, the method of conflict resolution emerged. Chris Lamn, a childcare instructor from Fullerton Community College in California, conducted a unique project that demonstrates this concept—Peace Camp. In a summer program, children from five to ten years of age were given tools for resolving conflict. When someone was upset, fighting, or irritated with another child, they would sit at the peace table, where a teacher would say, "Okay, what is going on?" When the children explained their situation, they were asked, "So, what do you think will solve this situation?" After they each came up with a solution, they were instructed to try one. They were expected to report back in a short time to evaluate the procedure taken. It was observed that the children eventually would approach each other and say, "Hey, let's figure out what we can do here."

The Effect of Negative and Positive Spirals

I am sure you are thinking, that's great, but how does this apply on the homefront? To begin with, toddlers (ages one to two and a half) need redirection, like pointing out something else to do, because they are limited in their ability to communicate. When preschool-age children (two to four) misbehave, they usually respond when you eliminate a favorite activity. But think about this strategy. Basic classical conditioning suggests that rewards work better than punishments, and intangible rewards like praise surpass tangible rewards like food or gifts. It would, therefore, make the most sense to honor good behavior consistently in the preschool years. Lean down and tell your child your expectation. Get down to his level; be gentle yet firm. It's not about punishment at this age. It is about guiding him to see another outcome like loving his friend rather than hitting him so that his friend can love him back. Say, "I know you can play nicely so that your friend will play nicely with you." This concept may be challenging, but it is just something you need to work at. When you stay upbeat and positive, your child will learn to self-regulate his own behavior.

Later, when children are able to communicate (around age four), conflict resolution begins to work. Time-out does not teach a child what to do after everyone cools down. It can turn into a negative spiral because of resentment. Conflict resolution, however, works on a positive spiral.

Even with these basic age parameters, other factors need to be considered, such as temperament, gender, the environment, and the time of the experience. Here is an example of using conflict resolution at home. My sister-in-law, Jeanne, has two sons who are eighteen months apart, Mike and Bobby. They were always scrapping as young boys. Since I have girls, I was intrigued by how Jeanne handled the more aggressive situations with her boys. When they came to her crying, she would get at eye level and say to each one, "Okay, what happened?" After each one explained his side of the situation, she would say, "So how can you work this out?" Both boys would come up with some suggestions. Then Jeanne would say, "Let's try doing it this way and see what happens." By then the tears were dry and they would go to play again. At the time, I had never heard of conflict resolution. All I knew was that Jeanne instinctively knew how to defuse a situation as well as how to teach her sons tolerance and acceptance.

Successful companies today use conflict resolution. When there is a stressful situation, workers are asked for their input, and new ways of doing things emerge within an arena of trust and respect. Conflict resolution works for children as long as they are able to communicate. If they learn this skill at a young age, they are more likely to be respectful as they grow into their teens and beyond.

Even when my daughters, who got into situations very different from those of my nephews, were older, *redirection* often worked. My husband called their form of scrapping "touch and whine." For example, one summer we took a family road trip. Sharri and Amy, who were three years apart, were in the back seat touching, poking, and crying. After awhile, my husband said, "Hey, let's play a new game called *the silent game*. Let's see who can be quiet the longest." We looked at each other and smiled because we knew silence wouldn't last long. Then we would pull over at the next rest stop and let the girls run around. We also sang songs and played games, like looking for different state license plates or signs with different letters, always *redirecting* their behavior. Today we have earphones so everyone can listen to their own music and even DVD players for showing movies in the back seat of the car. Unfortunately, this is not as interactive, stimulating, or creative. Child development specialist Michael Leeman urges us not to promote this type of separation via technology. Children's memories depend on singing, talking, and playing games. I believe we have to understand that in certain situations, like long car rides, we must accept the limited abilities of our children's underdeveloped nervous systems. By being patient and accepting, along with your own personal creativity, you will give your children magical moments as well as teach them positive discipline.

Figure 5 describes some of the criteria of negative and positive spirals.

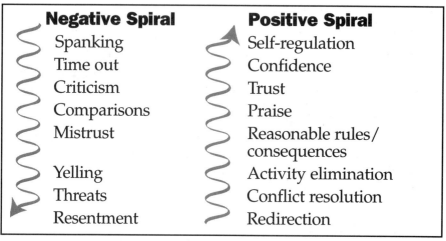

Negative Spiral	Positive Spiral
Spanking	Self-regulation
Time out	Confidence
Criticism	Trust
Comparisons	Praise
Mistrust	Reasonable rules/ consequences
Yelling	Activity elimination
Threats	Conflict resolution
Resentment	Redirection

Figure 5. Negative and Positive Spirals

Then They Become Teenagers

A current child development specialist, Dr. Becky Bailey, defines misbehavior in this quote. I see the intent of dealing with teenagers in her words.

> Most of the misbehavior children exhibit is children just being children. Children must test the limits. It is their job description. Through this testing, they discover the boundaries of life. They discover what is and what is not acceptable behavior in certain situations. Just as a child cannot attain a real notion of the size, color and characteristics of an elephant only by reading about them, so children cannot be told something is "wrong" without experiencing it directly. That is just the way it is. This constant and repeated testing can be trying even to the most patient parents.[6]

Disciplining teenagers is very different from disciplining younger children. Here is where "testing the limits" is exhibited to the maximum. This is where parents, as explained in Chapter 3, deal with a lot of stress in their personal relationships. A consistent lifestyle helps families with teenagers—same parents, same home, same school, and same friends. Also, by now, both parents should have had time to explore their passions, reach their educational competencies, and have fulfilling, meaningful work.

However, the perception of what *should* happen is not necessarily the real-life experience of many families. Parents often get divorced, are single, or are starting new relationships. Teenagers are limited in understanding their parents' emotional needs and many times focus on the divorce as being unfair to them. Some families have to endure other changes like moving, thus disrupting school and friendship experiences. Many parents are still searching for the right job and equitable financial compensation. And if these life struggles aren't enough, add to this complicated mess the raging, hormonal boost of testosterone and estrogen flying everywhere, peer pressure to do drugs, overcrowded schools, and part-time jobs.

What is a parent of teenagers to do? Here are some guidelines to support families of teenagers who are struggling:

1. Seek personal fulfillment in your relationship and your work

2. Be consistent with a balanced parenting style, as explained in Chapter 2

3. Support your teenager emotionally and financially while he seeks what he wants to do for the rest of his life

4. Clearly communicate daily schedules

5. Practice reasonable rules and consequences for learning appropriate, respectful behavior

6. Take time to go on family outings and just have fun together

REFLECTIVE EXERCISE

Close your eyes and take a deep breath. Visualize yourself in a place of calm. Know that your love will help with your future discipline situations. Know you have children with great behavior and that you listen to them and respect their feelings. Realize that you are there to love and be a good example for your children. Be thankful that you have the gift of strength to discipline them.

Chapter Activities

In your workbook you will find the following activities:

- List of discipline techniques you have been using
- Communication agreement
- Plan to achieve good behavior

In the next chapter, you will learn what to expect as your children learn.

It would be the greatest of tragedies if now,
in the midst of the golden age of brain/mind research,
when we are discovering the full range of what we contain
and what we yet may be, we agree to a limited vision of our
possibilities amped up with new technologies.

~*Dr. Jean Houston*[1]

Learning

When I watch a butterfly . . . I learn
When the sun sets behind the water's edge . . . I learn
When I see a child cry . . . I learn
When his eyes are wiped by Mom . . . I learn

When you take my hand . . . I learn
When you yell at me . . . I learn
When you read me a story . . . I learn
When I watch TV . . . I learn

When I see you go to work . . . I learn
When I see you take a drink . . . I learn
When you show me how to fish . . . I learn
When you clean the house and paint the porch. . . I learn
and when you pray with me at night . . . I learn.

All I am, all I do, I learn by watching, by watching you.

~ *Christine L. Assad*

CHAPTER 6

Learning

Where We Are Now

The other day, I met a lovely young mother at a social gathering. She mentioned that her daughter's school has a computer at every desk. I responded by saying, "That's really great but also sad. Schools should be preparing kids for life, not to work on computers." As we talked further, she began to understand my perspective. Where are the art projects? Where are the music lessons? Where are the hands-on interactive experiences? How can children gain life skills through two-dimensional sources like computers?

As a high school child development teacher, I am acutely aware of the ever-present disregard for hands-on, or kinesthetic, learning. Recently our on-site childcare center was dismantled to make room for a new science building, which will be great, but why can't we have a new science building on one side of the school and a childcare facility on the other?

It is not just childcare or the other school training programs that are in jeopardy. Art, music, drama, dance, cooking, sewing, woodshop, and automotive classes are often disregarded because of the academic push. Everything in education today focuses on the almighty exam scores. Communities are pitted against each other to see which district can produce the highest scores, which are printed in the local papers for everyone to see. The perception is that all parents want their children to go to college and work in business. If that were to happen, who would build the houses, fix the cars, build roads, and do the plumbing? And let us not forget those people who create aesthetic works in art, music, drama, and dance. People also need to cook, design clothing, and work in childcare centers. In our communities, we need to examine the focus we want for our children. Getting a college education is great, but without electives to stimulate passion and creativity in our children, what's the point? The answer is *balance.* We should strive for both excellent academics and terrific electives.

Where Education Has Been

The educational strategy used for centuries has been *information processing.* It has been the accepted way to learn. Teachers give information, children practice, and teachers test. In other words, information is received into the memory. How long it stays there depends on how much repetition or practice the student gets. The more exposure information gets, the longer it is retained in the memory. Grades and competition emerged over the years supposedly to enhance the *importance* of the process. However, it has been observed that most significant memory comes from highly charged emotional events. For example, most people who were around in 1963 can tell you exactly when, where, and how they heard the news about President Kennedy's assassination. Another example is the World Trade Center and Pentagon attacks of September 11, 2001.

Here is a practical application of this concept. Remember when you were a child and you had to learn your spelling words for the week? What did you do to learn them? You probably relied on memorization. You wrote the words over and over again and a family member quizzed you while you ate your cereal on Friday morning. How did you usually do on the test? For many people this process was tedious and painful. Then there were the spelling bees. Did you hate doing that? Talk about embarrassing! It was open, on-the-spot competition in front of your peers. No stress there!

Dealing with Dyslexia

Standard information processing did not work for me as a child. For example, when there was a spelling bee, I would beg to be the scorekeeper. Many years later, when I was in my thirties, I realized that I am dyslexic. What that basically means is that I cannot hear the ever-so-slight variations in many of the sounds in our language. Spelling was and still is nearly impossible for me. I also would write my letters upside down and backwards. In fact, I still do. It baffled me as a child. It made me feel like I was less than the other children who were good at language skills. I struggled through school, often wondering what I would ever amount to if people really knew how stupid I was. But something inside told me that I would be all right. At one point in my life, the Dyslexia Association came to my assistance. I was told the facts about the condition. I learned that it is not an *intelligence* dysfunction. Actually, most dyslexic persons have average to above average IQs. In fact, many well-known people have been dyslexic: Albert Einstein, Walt Disney, Nelson Rockefeller, Bruce Jenner, and Tom Cruise, to name a few. It appears to be genetic, so if you identify with a troubled learning situation and your child is struggling in school, consider getting him tested for dyslexia. It affects about twenty percent of the population, yet most school districts do not know what to do with the children who are affected by this condition.[2] Children with dyslexia need a multisensory, or kinesthetic, experience to process information optimally. Tutoring from you or a specialist may help significantly. For further information about dyslexia, and how to help children who have it, log on to *www.dyslexia.org*. The point here is that *information processing* did not work well for me, and probably hasn't worked well for other dyslexic people either.

Different Types of Learners

Added to the arena of education are the following three different learning methods and the percentage of people in each one:[3]

Auditory	15 percent
Visual	40 percent
Kinesthetic	45 percent

Let's examine how these methods work with the *information processing* strategy. When children just hear the words, only fifteen percent of them receive the information easily; when they write the words, forty percent of them get it. That leaves forty-five percent of children needing a kinesthetic, or multisensory, way to learn. Unfortunately, traditional, verbal-based education does little to support children who need to learn this way. It seems that there is a connection to dyslexic children, as well. I like what Jean Houston tells us:

> A child can learn math as a rhythmic dance, and learn it well, for rhythm is processed in the brain in areas adjacent to the centers for pattern and order. A child can learn almost anything if she is dancing, tasting, touching, hearing, seeing, and feeling information. She becomes a passionate learner who delights in using much more of her mind/brain/body system than conventional schooling generally permits. Much of the failure in schools stems from boredom, which arises from the system's longer failure to stimulate and not repress those wonder areas in a child's brain that give her so many ways of responding to the world.[4]

Not too long ago, I was visiting my friend's second grade classroom. She was having her students write their spelling words and put them into sentences. I suggested that they draw a picture of the words. My friend agreed that this was a good idea. The children were excited about this different approach to learning their spelling words. Your child's teacher may or may not know that children may do better by trying different ways to learn. Be responsible and ask your child's teacher to try various approaches to learning so that kinesthetic children have the same opportunity to learn. You can also try multiple approaches at home to make a difference in your child's ability to learn.

The Chavez family of Albuquerque, New Mexico, did just that. A recent news article about them reported that all five of their children graduated from Harvard and have excellent, meaningful adult careers. The basic things they did to achieve this were:

1. They restricted television watching to two hours a week; extra time was spent reading books and encyclopedias

2. They played classical music in the house and provided lessons in violin, classical guitar, and piano, as well as other enrichment activities

3. They taught their children math, geography, and reading before they even started school

4. They paid what scholarships didn't cover to get their children into the best prep schools in town

5. They were always communicating with their children about what they were doing at school and during their free time

The parents, Ray and Rosario Chavez, were committed to giving their children an excellent education. This couple, with a modest income, was awarded a special plaque signed by the dean of Harvard University, which reads: "To Ramon and Rosario Chavez—Harvard expresses its respect, admiration, and thanks for the gift of their five extraordinary children."[5] Now think back to our parenting quadrants. Where is the Chavez family? It's hard to say with such a small amount of information, but they were definitely committed and together on a positive spiral.

Where Are We Going?

To help you understand how children learn, let's look at what researchers have found in the twentieth century and what they are discovering today. The most famous researcher in the twentieth century was Jean Piaget, known as the Father of Child Development. In his fifty years of research, between the 1930s and the 1980s, he observed that children learn in four stages, one building upon the other:

Stage 1	0 to 2 years	Sensorimotor
Stage 2	3 to 5 years	Preoperational
	< 5-to-7 shift >	
Stage 3	5 to 12 years	Concrete Operational
Stage 4	12 years and up	Formal Operational

In Stage 1, or the Sensorimotor stage, babies learn by putting things into their mouths, touching and feeling everything in sight. They also repeat an action that gets a response. When they shake a rattle, they are rewarded with a sound. Modern manufacturers of children's toys have learned to market this principle. It is rare to find a new stuffed toy that doesn't talk or giggle back to a child when it is squeezed. Piaget referred to this stage as the time of the little scientist. While sitting in a high chair, a child may drop something and notice a sound. Then she may drop something else to see if it makes the same or a different sound. She isn't trying to drive her parents crazy by making a mess all over the floor.

Stage 2 is the Preoperational stage. Piaget found that young children see only one aspect of something at a time. He developed a reliable, or repeatable, method of testing called *conservation,* which has been done on thousands of children all over the world. Perhaps you have heard of the following classic example. You fill two short, fat glasses with the same amount of water. You show the child that the glasses have the same amount of water. Then you say, "Now watch what happens when I put the water of one glass into a tall, skinny glass. Which glass has more water?" The child between three to five years of age will say the tall, skinny glass has more water. Why? Because it appears like there is more to the young child. The visual perception is more than the actual understanding of quantity of the water.

The results of Piaget's conservation testing led him to conclude that teaching sounds of the alphabet to youngsters under five years old is just about impossible. I interpret it this way. Think of all the variations of the English alphabet. The letter A alone has three sounds: short, long, and in-between (the one with the two dots over it). Here is the example I use: The angel (long A) ate an  apple (short A), and flew away (in-between A). As you can see, there are many aspects to analyze. A is not the only letter that can be pronounced in more than one way.

Between Stages 2 and 3 is the 5-to-7 Shift, or the in-between-land for children. When doing the classic water conservation task, a child at this stage would say, "If you put the water back in the short, fat glass, the water is the same." Piaget called this *reversing*. Some children understand the concept that A has three sounds, and some do not. His understanding of the stages emphasized the importance of waiting to teach reading until age seven, when it is far easier for all children to grasp the complexities of language.

Stage 3 is the Concrete Operational stage. Piaget said that children between five and twelve need to touch or operate concrete things in order to learn. In other words, he did not believe that children should learn the difference between halves and wholes by looking at a demonstration on paper, a two-dimensional experience. He said teachers need real items for their students to touch and compare. As Piaget's teachings became accepted in the 1980s, teachers wanted kits to go with their textbooks, so businesses began to market such products. One famous example is a teaching strategy called "Math Their Way." In this system, students count each day they are at school with tangible items, like beads. Day ten is marked with a special tangible item; and so it continues to day 100, when they have a 100 party. Groups of ten things are all over the classroom and students count to ten in each group with different tangible items. Sometimes edible goodies, like marshmallows and M&Ms, are used to add to the fun. This is usually done in a kindergarten classroom. Unfortunately, hands-on learning is neglected as children get older and teachers fall back into the old language-based, information-processing learning strategy.

Stage 4 is the Formal Operational stage. Piaget saw this stage as a time when children are ready to grasp the abstract—word problems in math, finding the unknown in algebra, and the social complexities of bias.[6] Many American schools jump into this type of advanced learning before age twelve and then wonder why students sometimes find school beyond their grasp.

New Ways for Children to Learn

While Piaget's conservation and other tests were reliable (repeated over and over by different children), they were not valid. Critics of Piaget pointed out that children were influenced by the way they were asked the questions.[7] Consequently, the new army of researchers needed to do more to establish valid reasons why children learn. In the 1990s, a professor at Harvard, Dr. Howard Gardner, expanded the horizon of learning. With new modern technologies based on physical evidence of brain functioning, he has identified *eight intelligences* of the brain. They are listed in Figure 6 along with how children learn.[8]

People are excited about this research. Now, when administrators cut electives, teachers can say, "Hey, wait a minute. Look at this research." Unfortunately, this is like preaching to the

Logical/Mathematical	learn by reasoning solutions
Linguistic	learn by verbalizing
Kinesthetic	learn by touch and movement
Visual/Spatial	learn through visual symbols
Musical	learn through beat and rhythm
Interpersonal	learn by sensing the feelings of others
Intrapersonal	learn by awareness of one's own feelings
Naturalistic	learn through awareness of environment

Figure 6. Eight Intelligences of the Brain

choir. The principals and superintendents know all the theories, old and new. They are in survival mode themselves. It's the parents and taxpayers who want the academics. In other words, it's the prevailing consciousness of the time we live in right now.

I cannot possibly leave my favorite teacher of child development out of this chapter. Her name is Bev Bos, and she really has been my teacher only through her workshops and books. She is known for her imagination, her insights into the human spirit, her intelligence, and her sense of humor. I have attended more than twenty of her workshops over the last twenty-five years and have had the good fortune to spend some quality time with her as well as to receive many of her famous hugs. It is like she just keeps me going.

What I have learned from Bev and her wonderful son-in-law, Michael Leeman, a child development specialist as well, is that children are so very precious and deserve the most profound respect. She believes that kids need *wonder, discovery, and experience* to learn and that they need to have safe play with an illusion of risk. How else will they be prepared for this world? She believes passionately that children learn through play, that they need to be prepared for tough experiences, like death, and that childhood needs to be special beyond belief, so that they will have exceptional memories to sustain them for the rest of their lives. I urge all of you parents to see her if she comes to your town. If nothing else, read her latest book, *Falling Over the Edge*, which she wrote with her friend Jenny Chapman. You can find out more about Bev Bos at her Web site: *www.turnthepage.com*.

I want to share with you a statement from Dr. Carla Hannaford, another profound teacher:

> We are still leaning too heavily on algorithmic (linear, mathematical, rule-oriented) learning, still expecting students to learn primarily through rote memorization, all the way up through college. Why? Memory and linear skills are easy to test and quantify. These kinds of tests give objective comparisons. But what do they measure? Facts and linear skills are useful acquisitions, but are they the most important part of a person's education? Shouldn't we be more concerned about thinking, creativity, application of knowledge to real life situations? The emphasis on low-level skill and memory testing fosters an emphasis on low-level thought processing—teaching to tests. Consequently, practice in high-level thinking can be and often is shortchanged.[9]

Get Proactive

So now we have another respected person in the field of cognitive development lamenting the current atrocities of the learning system. What can be done to get everyone on track, headed down the path of respect for ability, equality of opportunity, as well as enrichment of the spirit within each and every child? Parents need to get involved with their children's education. Home schooling works for some people, but most of us need to support the systems available to us. Volunteer to help in your child's classroom. Join the PTA. Go to school board meetings. Write letters to your district superintendents. Send a letter to the editor or your local paper. Call your state and federal legislators. Let everyone know you want optimal teaching through all the learning modalities. Fight to keep electives. Talk to your neighbors and friends about providing exceptional education opportunities at your schools. It takes more than the basic three R's—reading, writing, and arithmetic. Vote for the bond issues that involve hands-on learning: science labs, drama programs, music, and art programs. Support the creative curricula in the charter schools near you. In your own family, commit to excelling like Ray and Rosario Chavez. Be aware that your child's whole brain and body need to be involved in his evolving spirit.

Marion Wright Edelman, director of the Children's Defense League, makes this challenge:

> Assign yourself. My Daddy used to ask us whether the teacher had given us any homework. If we said no, he'd say, "Well, assign yourself." Don't wait around for your boss or your co-worker or spouse to direct you to do what you are able to figure out and do for yourself. Don't do just as little as you can to get by. If someone asks you to do A, and B and C obviously need to be done as well, do them without waiting to be asked or expecting a Nobel prize for doing what is needed. Too often today too many ordinary, thoughtful deeds are treated as extraordinary acts of valor. Democracy is not a spectator sport. Vote. And don't hide behind the excuse that one vote doesn't count. Don't just complain about our political leaders; run for political office, especially school boards. Those with a special commitment to children and families and the needy have a special role to play in public life. But please don't think that your position or your re-election are the only point once you gain office. Children are. Results are. If you see a need, don't ask, "Why doesn't somebody do something?" Ask, "Why not do something?" Do not wait around to be told what to do. There is nothing more wearing than people who have to be asked or reminded to do things

repeatedly. Hard work, initiative and persistence are still the non-magic carpets to success. Let's each commit to help teach the rest of the country how to achieve again by our example.[1]

Close your eyes and take a deep breath. Visualize your children educated to their greatest potential. Know that they will blossom and grow in their educational process with perfect support from caregivers and teachers. Be thankful for your own abilities as well as those involved with your children's educations.

Chapter Activities

In your workbook you will find the following activities:

- Howard Gardner Questionnaire and evaluation
- Plan to enrich and educate your children

In the next chapter, you will learn what your role is in the moral development of your children.

Freedom is indivisible;
the chains on only one of my people
were the chains on all of them,
the chains on all of my people
were the chains on me.
~ *Nelson Mandela*[1]

The Subconscious Mind

I wanna hit my brother sometimes . . . he'll survive.
I wanna pinch my sister . . . she will only whine.
Sometimes it's okay if I take something small, like a candy bar at
the drugstore or some clothes at the mall.
Nobody will know.

But then, when I was working at the snack shack, I didn't charge
my friend for his chips. My boss saw and told me to leave due
to my crime.
And then, my friend who sold drugs to make his car payment got
caught.
The law picked him up and he is now serving time.

Maybe being bad is not so good.
Maybe I should be good and care if I hurt someone.
Maybe I should not take things that are not mine.

I think I can put aside my anxiety and help others to be good, like
the kids in the neighborhood.
I think I can learn to forgive and work with others to turn the world
into a better place.
I think I can be an example to others that love and caring is what
really matters.
I think I can. I know I can. And I will.

~D. H. Summers

Parenting Outside the Box

CHAPTER 7

Morals

Who's Cheating Today's Teenagers?

In June, 2002, Christine Pelton, a high-school teacher at Piper High School in Piper, Kansas, quit her job, along with the principal and thirteen of the thirty-two teachers at the school. The reason was *cheating*. Twenty-eight sophomores were caught cheating by Ms. Pelton. This biology teacher confirmed that 28 of her 118 students had copied each other's assignment in a cut-and-paste manner, which was clearly against guidelines that had been set forth. Even though the teacher, Ms. Pelton, had explicitly defined plagiarism in her syllabi, signed by both parents and students, the students still cheated. This assignment was one-half of their grade, and they all got zeros, which affected their grades, their GPAs, and their chances to be accepted into good colleges. Outraged parents badgered the school board to order Ms. Pelton to change her decision. She was enraged when the students actually cheered the fact that she was being portrayed in a negative fashion. She quit her job before lunch.[2]

This incident was reported on national news, and people were bewildered by the unethical standards to which our nation has apparently fallen. If you consider the cheating recently discovered in large public corporate scandals, like Enron's bookkeeping atrocities and Merrill Lynch's practice of recommending junk stock, is it any surprise that students don't think it's unimportant if they copy each other's work?

What I see being demonstrated by this example in Kansas is a dichotomy that people have between fear of failure and self-confidence. To examine why fear can cause a lack of self-confidence, let's look at how moral development emerges, according to the experts.

Moral Development

Lawrence Kohlberg, the recognized authority of moral development, did some amazing work from 1963 to 1981. He came up with six stages of moral development based, in part, on answers he received from eighty-four boys to questions concerning a life-and-death moral dilemma.

> A woman in Europe was near death from cancer. One drug might save her, a form of radium that a druggist in the same town had recently discovered. The druggist was charging $2,000, ten times what the drug cost him to make. The sick woman's husband, Heinz, went to everyone he knew to borrow money, but could get together only about half of what it cost. He told the druggist that his wife was dying and asked him to sell it cheaper or let him pay later. But the druggist said "No." The husband was desperate and broke into the man's store to steal the drug for his wife. If you were the husband, would you have done that? Why?[3]

The data Kohlberg collected from responses to this dilemma established the following stages of moral development:

Stage 1   Might makes right
Stage 2   Look out for number one
Stage 3   Good girl and nice boy
Stage 4   Law and order
Stage 5   Social contract, emphasis is on accepted moral principals
Stage 6   Universal ethical principle, beyond what has been accepted

I will merge Kohlberg's stages with concepts from Dr. Marcia Sutton and Dr. Lloyd Strom's book, *Kingdoms of Creation: A Map Of Spiritual Growth*,[4] which are as follows:

- The Search—Seat of Self-Awareness

- The Quickening—Seat of Self-Actualization

- The Gathering—Seat of Self-Recognition

- The Prize—Seat of Self-Revelation

Follow with me the progress of moral development, because essentially your own moral development will guide your child's spirit. The higher you go, the higher they will go.

In my interpretation, I call my examples the Rooms of Moral Development. I also coordinate the parenting styles from the quadrants in Chapter 2 to fit the moral development of the parent.

Room 1 of Moral Development
Sutton and Strom: The Search—
Seat of Self-Awareness

Kohlberg's Stage 1—Might makes right; and Stage 2—Look out for number one

Emphasis is on getting rewards and avoidance of punishments.

Interpretation: An adult in these stages is overwhelmed by fear. He obeys only to avoid punishment. He is also looking out for himself and is in survival mode. If he feels he needs something, he may take it as long as he thinks he will not get caught.

Often a person in Room 1 is burdened with dysfunction. He feels everything is happening *"TO me."* With so much self-pressure, he has low self-esteem and often falls into self-abuse. I call these people *hand-wringers*.

As a parent, this person would be dysfunctional because his fear would run the family into dysfunctional behavior.

M o r a l   D e v e l o p m e n t

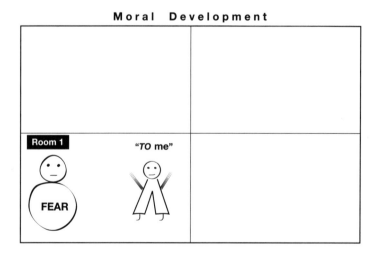

Room 2 of Moral Development
Sutton and Strom: The Quickening—
Seat of Self-Actualization

Kohlberg's Stage 3—Good girl and nice boy; and Stage 4—Law and order

Emphasis is on social rules.

Interpretation: To enter this room from the previous one, a person needs a life-altering experience like the death of a loved one, loss of a marriage, overcoming an addiction, and so on. This is often referred to as "the dark night of the soul." A person in this stage has less fear, but it still runs her life. She knows that she now has approval and is a good member of society, but she is not going beyond what she is able to do to make her own life better. Fear is not overwhelming, but it is still a prominent part of her life.

Often a person in this room is very decent and conscientious of what society expects of her. She feels that everything that she does is "*FOR* me." Going beyond her realm of comfort is not worth the extra effort.

As a parent, this person would need to be in control by being either very protective or the opposite, so deep into her self-need that she neglects her children.

Room 3 of Moral Development
Sutton and Strom: The Gathering—
Seat of Self-Recognition

Kohlberg's Stage 5—Social contract

Emphasis in on accepted moral principles.

Interpretation: To enter this room a person needs to have worked on his spiritual growth. Because of his strong foundation, he believes that if a standard or rule is broken, he needs to do something. Things should be right, even if effort is required. A person in this level has altruistic behavior. He thinks and acts for the good of others as well as himself. Honesty and good character are what a person at this stage is all about.

Often a person in this room knows that wonderful things can be done *"WITH me."*

There is a self-realization that with his effort, life can be better. A person in this room goes beyond his realm of comfort to improve the lives of others.

As a parent, this person would be balanced between control of and freedom for his children.

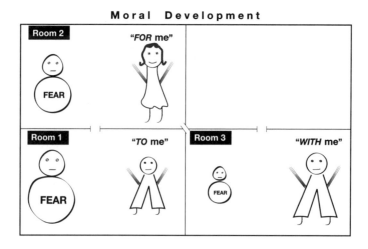

82

Room 4 of Moral Development
Sutton and Strom: The Prize—
Seat of Self-Revelation

Kohlberg's Stage 6—Universal ethical principles

Emphasis is on universal principles, beyond what has been accepted.

Interpretation: To enter this room a person has extraordinary passion. She devotes her life to improving the lives of others. No sacrifice is too great if the world will be improved by her efforts. There is no fear, only love and compassion in her life.

Often, a person in this room is considered to be exceptional, but fame is not a criterion. Everything about this person is done *"AS me;"* she is the model for others. Drawn by overwhelming consequence, she will even give her life to improving the lives of others.

This person actually may be so busy saving the world that she may sometimes neglect her own children. When she is with them, however, she will give them a balance of freedom, structure, and love.

Moral Development

Being a Role Model for Your Children

Figure 7 represents the four stages of moral development and their doors of passage.

Moral Development

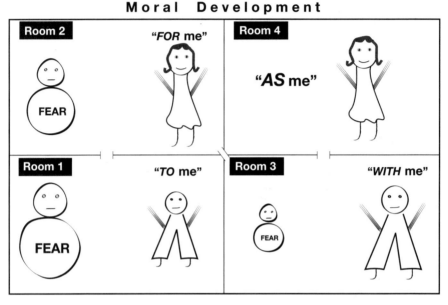

Figure 7. Four Stages of Moral Development

Kohlberg teaches us the moral standards of life. Drs. Sutten and Strum give us a spiritual guideline. By combining their thoughts, I see clarity of will and spirit for raising children. In Room 1, parents overwhelmed with fear may have kids who are unwilling to take risks. In Room 2, parents who provide only for their own needs might foster children who do not care about others. In Room 3, parents who go beyond the expected could possibly have kids who fly beyond what anyone can imagine. Kohlberg used examples like Mother Teresa, Martin Luther King, Nelson Mandela, and Mahatma Gandhi, in other words, Nobel Peace Prize winners for Room 4. These people are the ultimate example of having high moral standards, as they seem to have loved everyone as their children. Many people who are not so famous are also exceptional. Maybe you know one personally.

An interesting perspective on moral development emerges when you contrast humanness to spirituality. In Room 1, where everything happens *"TO me,"* human beings are having a human experience. In Room 2, where everything happens *"FOR me,"* human beings are having a spiritual experience. In Room 3, where everything happens *"WITH me,"* spiritual beings are having a human experience. Finally, in Room 4, where everything happens *"AS me,"* spiritual beings are having a spiritual experience. Figure 8 provides a perspective contrasting our human connection to our spirituality.

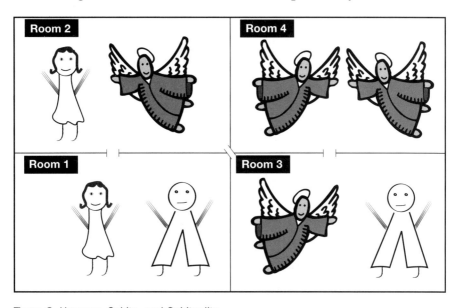

Figure 8. Humans, Spirits, and Spirituality

Stages of Grief

Often a crisis can occur in a family. Perhaps one child will be born with or develop a catastrophic condition or illness. Some examples would be: autism, Down's syndrome, leukemia, a brain tumor, or diabetes. On occasion, an accident has caused the sudden death of a child. When this happens, human nature releases a sense of grief. Elisabeth Kubler-Ross observed the following stages of grief: denial, anger, bargaining, depression, and acceptance.[5]

As a family is impacted by a catastrophe, it is important to continuously strive through the process. No matter how uncomfortable or how horrible your personal disaster, the experience is yours so that you have the opportunity to climb, crawl if you can, to the next stage of moral development. As Ram Dass says, "The dark night of the soul is when you have lost the flavor of life but not yet gained the fullness of divinity."[6] The "dark night," the horrible experience, is, in fact, your opportunity to grow closer to your spiritual source.

My daughter Sharri was exposed to a form of herpes in her seventh month of pregnancy. She noticed a significant lack of activity from the baby. Within a few days, an emergency C-section resulted in a dead baby. A seemingly unbearable experience penetrated her life. In time, Sharri found a support group for mothers who had lost their babies. For weeks and months, she shared her grief and torment to sympathetic women who provided lots of tissues for her tears, along with warmth and understanding. It was so sad for me to watch her go through the denial, anger, bargaining, and depression. I could see that the hurdle to acceptance was hard. I took her on a weekend trip and explained to her how the death of her baby, Jacob, was a special lesson of love from God. We talked about how every doctor and nurse in that operating room was crying when Jacob could not even take one breath of life. I just know that everyone who even heard about Jacob's death in the hospital that day went home and hugged their own children a little tighter and gave them a little more love in honor of the tragic loss of Jacob. His very existence, even for a brief time, taught everyone about love. Everyone who supported her was getting a lesson in love. Sharri listened. Eventually, she became the source of warmth and understanding to the new mothers in the support group. Sharri started to pass out tissues for the tears of others.

Since then, Sharri has had another healthy baby, which is wonderful. But above all, with forgiveness she achieved acceptance and in the process raised her level of moral development. She is now in Room 3, a spiritual being having a human experience.

Shop for Your Spiritual Source

Achieving moral development does not always happen through crisis, and it does not come automatically. It takes effort. It helps to be with others who feel like you do about life. Often parents fall in love and have children before they ever realize a need for a spiritual source. Perhaps they were raised with different traditions and value systems. Maybe one or the other took a break from going to a place of worship in their young adult years and have just not yet returned. Then again, maybe the established religion of their youth has changed, or they have changed so that the old established religion does not feel right any more. Whatever the reason, a family needs to shop for a place to "fill the well," or replenish their souls. It may be easier than they think. Then again, maybe nothing will seem to be the right fit. If this happens, commit to spending time as a family in a special way to reconnect with your spiritual selves. My first husband said that he felt spiritually fulfilled when he was in the forest, so we often went on camping trips, breathing fresh mountain air and watching the stars from our sleeping bags. These were indeed spiritual moments.

A very simple thing to do to enhance moral development is to provide spiritual books for your children. Bedtime reading is magical anyway, and when they are older, it is great to be reading wonderful stories. Check the workbook for a list of spiritual books I really like, or check our web page, *www.summervillespirit.com.*

Morals by Example

Gary Zukav explains: "Non-judgmental justice is the freedom of seeing what you see and experiencing what you experience without responding negatively."[7] As parents, it is essential to give moral examples to your children. Let's say you are driving with your children in the car and someone of a different race cuts you off. Do you make a derogatory remark about the person's race under your breath? Do you get verbally angry? Children notice. As a childcare provider for years, I have been amazed at how many three-year-old children demonstrate extreme anger and, in some cases, even use profanity. Where did they learn these things?

Sometimes parents may feel that complaining about their work or the people they work for is okay to do in front of their children. If the experience is disruptive to your personal integrity, it is not all right. If your situation at work is not good, you should think about moving on to do something else.

Then again, some parents may feel it is okay to use illegal drugs or even buy and sell them to help pay for the rent or mortgage.

Children are smarter than you sometimes think, and they learn a lot through observation. Remember, your children are watching what you do and say. You are the foundation of their moral development. Don Miguel Ruiz tells us, "Impeccability of the word can lead you to personal freedom, to huge success and abundance; it can take away all fear and transform it into joy and love."[8] Just think! When you give your children good examples, they can begin life with an elevated moral development. Figure 9 on page 93 illustrates the big connection between moral development and the parenting quadrants.

Looking Outside the Box
Combining the Parenting Quadrants with Moral Development

One day I realized the huge impact represented in Figure 9 where I have combined the four parenting quadrants with the four rooms of moral development.

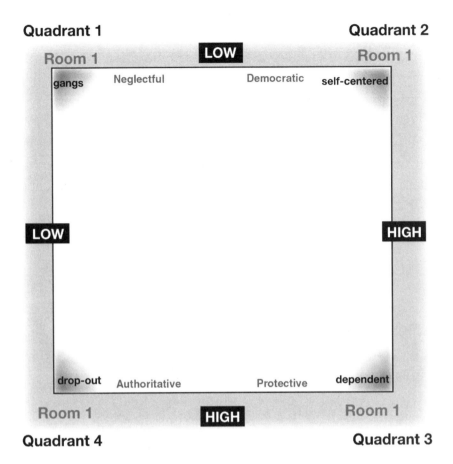

Quadrant 1

Room 1

LOW

gangs Neglectful

Quadrant 2

Room 1

Democratic self-centered

LOW

HIGH

drop-out Authoritative

Protective dependent

Room 1

HIGH

Room 1

Quadrant 4

Quadrant 3

Room 1

The gray outer edge represents Room 1 of moral development, which is fear-based and dysfunctional. Think of what the word *edgy* means. The children in these families feel on the edge because everything bad is happening *"TO me."* They react by joining gangs, acting self-centered, being dependent, and avoiding their responsibilities.

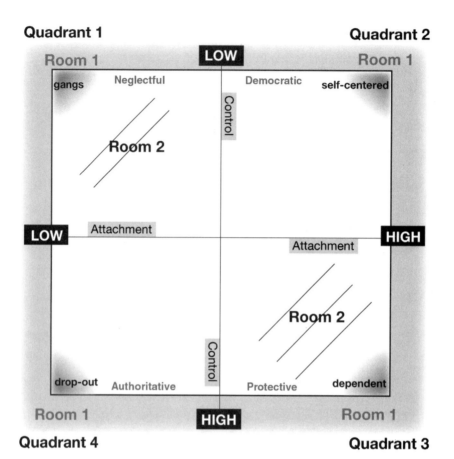

Quadrant 1

Quadrant 2

Room 1 — LOW — Room 1

gangs   Neglectful   Democratic   self-centered

Control

Room 2

LOW — Attachment — HIGH

Attachment

Room 2

Control

drop-out   Authoritative   Protective   dependent

Room 1 — HIGH — Room 1

Quadrant 4

Quadrant 3

Room 2

The striped lines in Quadrant 1, Neglectful, and Quadrant 3, Protective, represent Room 2 of moral development, which has less fear but does not reach out to help others. The children in these families feel everything is happening *"FOR me"* only. They react by doing only what is necessary for themselves. They will go to school, pass their classes, and maybe work part time, but they will not do any extra activities.

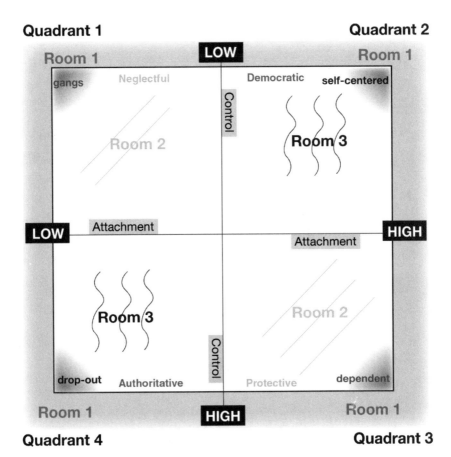

Quadrant 1 ... **Quadrant 2**

Room 1 — LOW — Room 1

gangs | Neglectful | Democratic | self-centered

Room 2 | Room 3

LOW — Attachment | Attachment — HIGH

Room 3 | Room 2

drop-out | Authoritative | Protective | dependent

Room 1 — HIGH — Room 1

Control

Quadrant 4 ... **Quadrant 3**

Room 3

The curved lines in Quadrant 2, Democratic, and Quadrant 4, Authoritative, represent Room 3 of moral development, which has very little fear and where reaching out to the community is expected. The children in these families will join sports or be in clubs at school and in the community. They believe that everything good is happening *"WITH me."*

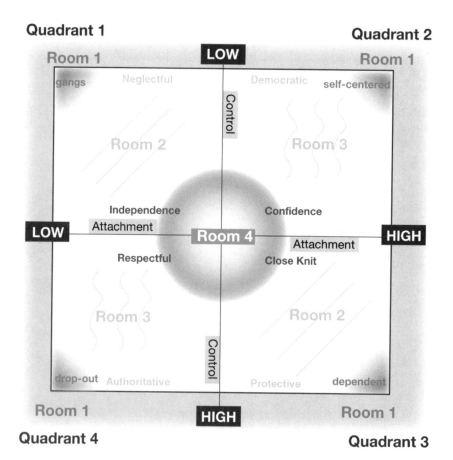

Quadrant 1

Room 1

LOW

Quadrant 2

Room 1

gangs   Neglectful   Democratic   self-centered

Control

Room 2   Room 3

Independence   Confidence

LOW   Attachment   Room 4   Attachment   HIGH

Respectful   Close Knit

Room 3   Room 2

Control

drop-out   Authoritative   Protective   dependent

Room 1

HIGH

Quadrant 4

Room 1

Quadrant 3

Room 4

The gray ball in the center represents Room 4 of moral development, which is love-based and absent of fear. The children in these families learn early that charity work and being totally aware of the needs of others is important. They believe that good can happen "*AS me.*" These children get good grades, take time for sports or extra activities, and represent themselves in a positive manner wherever they go. These children show independence and self-confidence. They are close-knit or friendly with everyone and are respectful of both themselves and others.

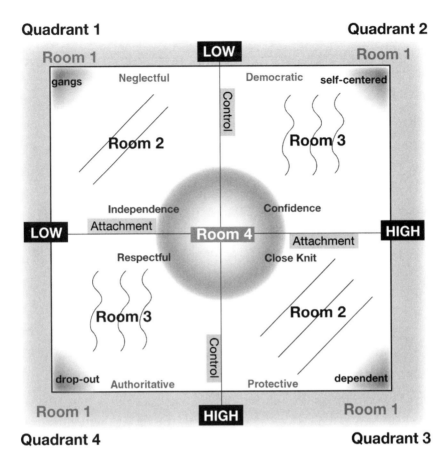

Figure 9. Moral Development and the Parenting Quadrants

The Three Big Issues

The biggest issues in life are relationships, finances, and health. Dealing with these aspects of our lives is a source of fear for many. Will this or that work? The best way to handle life's challenges is to approach them with a positive attitude. Know that everything will work out for the best. When we are faced with a terrible problem we often say, "It's for the best," or "When one door closes another opens." These statements can be aggravating at times. When you are in anguish, you are miserable. However, if you hang in there with a positive attitude, you will see how the change you fought turned out to be a friend. Often we turn to prayer in times of crisis. Talking to your spiritual source is a good thing. Better yet, try the eastern tradition of meditating, which really just means listening. After praying, be quiet and listen. What messages do you feel coming from inside of you? Some people say they have a gut feeling about something or their intuition leads them to where they need to go. I believe in making positive affirming statements. Say, "I know I will have a wonderful day." Speak and listen to your divine energy for guidance and you cannot go wrong. Tell your children, "I know you will do the best you can." Project love, because in the end that is all that really matters. Warren Hanson beautifully expresses love in this quote from his children's book, *The Next Place*:

> I will travel empty-handed. There is not a single thing I have collected in my life that I would ever want to bring except the love of those who loved me, and the warmth of those who cared. The happiness and memories and magic that we shared.
>
> Though I will know the joy of solitude, I'll never be alone. I'll be embraced by all the family and friends I've ever known. Although I might not see their faces, all our hearts will beat as one, and the circle of our spirits will shine brighter than the sun.
>
> I will cherish all the friendship I was fortunate to find, and the love and all the laughter in the place I leave behind. All these good things will go with me. They will make my spirit glow.
>
> And that light will shine forever in the next place that I go.[9]

Close your eyes and take a deep breath. Visualize yourself releasing fear and accepting all the love in your life. Know that you can provide a spiritual source for your children. See yourself as modeling the moral behavior that will give your children understanding of positive energy. Be grateful in your ability to achieve these things.

Chapter Activities

In your workbook you will find the following activities:

- Reflection of a person you know who has high moral development
- Plan for your own moral development
- Plan for the moral development of your children

In the next chapter, you will learn how balanced nutrition and a healthy environment will enhance your family.

Parenting Outside the Box

Good health should not be thought of as the absence of disease.
We should avoid this negative disease-oriented thinking
and concentrate on what we must do to remain healthy.

~ *Rod Burreson*[1]

The Nutrition Nut

People think you're nuts when you have passion about nutrition.

When I was a kid and my grandparents were always talking about nutrition, I thought they were nuts.

As a kid, I was on a quest to find the best candy bar in the world. I decided it was a Baby Ruth.

As a teenager, my idea of lunch was a bag of corn chips and an orange juice bar.

As a young parent, all I cared about was that the food was clean and fresh, and that my family liked it.

Now that I'm a grandparent, I have life experience. I know the value of each healthy day.

I have learned the importance of good nutrition, and now everyone thinks I'm nuts.

~D. H. Summers

Parenting Outside the Box

CHAPTER 8

Health

Big Concerns

With the high levels of fat, chemicals, and sugar in the American diet, health problems are increasing at a rapid rate. Obesity, diabetes, heart disease, and cancer are significant concerns that all parents should consider on a daily basis. The typical supermarket compounds the problem by stocking food items that have a long shelf life as well as food that tastes good. Processed foods like breads, crackers, chips, and cookies contain partially hydrogenated oils or trans-fatty acids to increase shelf life and make them taste better. Check the labels; it's amazing. These oils impact the cardiovascular system and play a part in creating fat in the body. The high sodium content of prepared foods is not good for the body, either. With the prevalence of convenience foods, families need to search for the freshest, most nutritious foods they can find (and also afford). One simple rule is, if God made it, you can eat it. However, to have healthy bodies we need to be aware of so much more.

Making Healthy Babies

Before you get pregnant, consider both your diet and use of toxic substances like alcohol, tobacco, and recreational drugs. A woman is born with all the eggs she will ever have, usually about 400 that survive to her adult years. Any illness she has or toxins she ingests affect her eggs, and her future children. A man produces new sperm every few days; however, men who use drugs or who work in toxic environments have been known to contribute to more miscarriages than men who do not. Remember, the healthier you are, the healthier your children will be. If you have been careless about your health and you want to become a parent, live a healthier lifestyle before trying to get pregnant. The benefits of this simple concept will be appreciated in time.

Physical Activity Guide For Your Children

Children need more exercise. School activities are great, if provided, but safe, physical experiences need to be available and affordable after school and on weekends, too. Here are four guidelines to physical development for formal play:

1. Children two to five years old need activities that use their bodies in space, such as gymnastics, dance, swimming, or karate.

2. Children five to eight years old need activities that use their bodies and a ball, like soccer, kick ball, and four square. Activities with a rope, like jump rope and tetherball, are good, too. Between these ages children can mentally and emotionally play games with simple rules.

3. Children eight years old and up have enough concentration to handle activities that use their bodies and a ball plus an an implement, such as golf, baseball, or tennis, which are also more mentally challenging.

4. At about ten years old, many children are more capable of physical endurance sports and activities like football, advanced ballet, and basketball. Also, competition is easier on them emotionally.

Without knowing this child-development sequence, parents involve their children in activities like baseball before their nervous systems are able to handle the eye-to-hand coordination needed for advanced sports. T-ball leagues for younger wannabe baseball players are fun for the parents, and some kids are darn good at an early age, but playing soccer may be more fun for the child to do first. These guidelines may help you understand an optimal progression to follow.

Informal play is important, too, and much cheaper. Playing at a park or discovering things in a big backyard can be great fun. If safety or remoteness is a problem, look for playgroups in your local paper. Get together with other parents and share responsibilities, while you make new adult friends at the same time.

Make a Difference

Another problem is the food offered at your children's school that might be somewhat grim. If you are not happy, call your district nutritionist and tell that person how you feel. I can just hear the reaction to your urges for organic products, but if you do not raise your school administration's consciousness, who will? I would be happy if just sodas and candy were eliminated from schools. Some courageous districts and even states are making proposals to their legislators to ban sodas and candy at school. At the high school where I teach, sodas, chips, and candy are the hot items. However, the staff tells me that healthier foods like ham and cheese sandwiches, milk, fruit drinks, water, and salads run out first because children really want to make healthier choices. Unfortunately, healthier foods have a shorter shelf life and are bought in less supply for fear that they will not be sold before they have to be thrown out.

Many times people object when "do-gooders" bring up the elimination of sodas and candy, because these items are often the catalyst for fund-raising for extra-curricular activities such as sports, band, and dance, that we all want to provide for our children. This is why better nutrition and enrichment activities are often at a standoff. I know that in time higher standards for healthy food and enrichment can co-exist. This balance must come from today's parents. So, parents, when you call, don't just complain, ask what you can do to provide better nutrition for your children.

So Much to Say, So Little Time

The twelve tips for optimal health on the next page are based on current research. Most of you probably already know some of this, and many of you are too busy to do the research. I've tried to make this as simple as possible. Copy it and put it on your refrigerator.

After all is said about optimal food choices, reality sets in when you send your children off to school. What can you pack that is nutritious and, at the very least, not harmful? You need to be aware of what is socially acceptable at your children's different age levels. Young children can be picky, and some moms are just happy that their children will eat anything. Older children are more conscious of what their friends think is weird or unusual. Some children would rather die than eat a banana at school. Here are some ideas to try. I would be really pleased if you would contact me and tell me how they work for you.

Packed Lunches for Young Children

Understand that using organic products is best.

Sandwiches

Raisin bread with cream cheese and jelly
Peanut butter (if not allergic) and jelly
Roast turkey and jellied cranberry slices
Provolone cheese and lettuce
Almond butter and banana
Tuna and chopped celery
Egg salad and shredded carrot
Bean and cheese burritos

12 Tips for Optimal Health

1. Do not eat peanut butter while you are pregnant, and avoid feeding it to children under the age of five.

2. Try to consume hormone-free meats and meat products.

3. Eat organic produce whenever possible. Wash all produce with vinegar and water. Eat in-season fruits and drink fruit juices in between meals for optimal digestion.

4. Drink bottled water: spring, reverse osmosis, or distilled. Get a water filter for the whole house.

5. Use only nontoxic soap and cleaning products.

6. Do not cook with aluminum foil or aluminum cookware. Use stainless steel cookware instead.

7. Be careful of fluoride use and dental fillings.

8. Use olive oil and avoid partially hydrogenated oils in processed foods.

9. Microwave your food in lead-free ceramic or glass containers. Never microwave in plastic containers.

10. Limit soda consumption.

11. Stay away from artificial diet products. Use natural sweeteners instead.

12. Take vitamins, minerals, and herbal supplements for good brain development, strong immune systems, and healthy bones.

Packing It Up

Use cool packs when possible for school lunches along with the following tips:

- Pack baby carrots, string cheese, or sliced apples in sealable sandwich bags and they will always be good to go

- Raw almonds are a great source of protein, last forever, and satisfy hunger pangs

- Pack small yogurt containers and juice boxes

- Good corn chips are the baked *organic* blue variety; they are more expensive but are much better than the other choices available

- If you are blessed with enough time to bake, small oatmeal cookies are good to include as well

- Encourage your children to save their fruit and fruit juices for mid-morning snack or to eat on the way home so that they get the most nutrition from their protein items

Follow what you can. Let the information in this chapter strengthen your knowledge to keep your family healthy.

Peanut Butter

Who would have thought that good old peanut butter would be a cause for concern? My step granddaughter, Yasmine, is five years old. Her first major episode with a peanut butter allergy resulted in instant vomiting and wheezing. Six months later, while making cookies with peanut butter in the dough, she broke out in hives accompanied by severe wheezing. This second episode also caused her face to swell for two days. The other day her preschool, which had been notified of her allergy, had a little party. Luckily, her mom was there to help and intervened as Yasmine was handed a peanut butter sandwich.

People are allergic to all kinds of things. I mention peanut butter because allergic reactions to it have increased over the past two decades. My research indicates that 1.1 percent of all children in the United States have an allergy to peanut butter. It can cause an anaphylactic reaction, which can even result in death. Two hundred children die each year from anaphylactic reactions, most of them from peanut butter. It appears that the dry-roasting or high-temperature processing of peanuts in the United States increases the allergenicity of the three major peanut proteins. One theory as to why the incidence of this allergy is increasing is the high use of peanut butter as a quick-energy food eaten by pregnant and lactating mothers. In addition, young children, who have immature immune systems, have difficulty fighting the dangers that these peanut proteins pose. Unfortunately, many children are exposed to peanut butter before their second birthday.[2]

Just to be safe, it's best not to eat peanut butter while pregnant or breast-feeding. Also, do not give babies, toddlers, or preschool children peanut butter until they are age five. If your child has a reaction, see an allergist and ask about having some epinephrine on hand in case of a severe reaction. Teachers and caregivers need to be extremely supportive of children with this allergy. Many preschools are establishing no-peanut-butter policies because of this situation.[3]

Hormones in Meat and Meat Products

Wholesome, natural milk is not as wholesome and natural as it used to be. Good old burgers are of concern, too. The reason: cows in the United States are given bovine growth hormones (BGH) to stimulate their production of milk. There is some concern that these hormones are not good for consumers.

According to Nathaniel Mead, "Back in 1987, the European Economic Community announced its plan to ban imports of meat treated with growth hormones because of suspected health hazards."[4] Since hormones stimulate growth of the entire body, there is strong evidence that, when consumed, they can metabolize and develop into breast cancer and possibly other cancers. The food given to the cows, which has a wide range of toxic and carcinogenic substances like pesticides, is also a source of concern. These toxins remain in the fat of cows and their dairy products. According to John McDougall, M.D., "Problems such as premature onset of maturity in men and women (along with premature menstruation and longer and more painful menstrual cycles) are associated with the hormonal effects of high-fat diets."[5]

Have you noticed how big some fifth graders are today? They are much more mature than children that age of long ago. When I was in high school in the 1960s, most of my friends did not start their periods until age thirteen to fifteen. Now, I am observing girls starting their periods between eight and eleven, and I am concerned about the health of children as it relates to their shortened childhoods. One solution is to buy organic milk and dairy products, as well as hormone-free meat, as often as possible. *Organic* means free of hormones or toxic chemicals. According to Lindsey Berkson, "Recently, consumers have been voting with their pocket-books, electing to pay more to protect their health by purchasing organic milk."[6] I noticed at my market that a private brand of organic milk, Horizon, was about thirty cents more per half gallon than the hormone-laden milk that was selling out. Now they have a store brand of organic milk for the same price as milk with hormones and it is always selling out. I have to go to a health food store to find organic butter, cottage cheese, and other organic milk products (the exception is Ben & Jerry's Ice Cream). This means that as a consumer, you have power. Demand organic dairy products and meat and, believe me, when enough people do, markets will sell it.

A great alternative to organic dairy products is goat's milk and cheese or feta. Goats are not injected with hormones, and the milk itself is easier to digest than cow's milk, which is good news for lactose-intolerant people. I was a little wary of tasting it myself. When I did, I was pleasantly surprised at its wonderful flavor.

Another choice might be soy milk. However, this product is controversial for children to consume due to both estrogenic (hormone) and goitrogenic (thyroid swelling) activities.[7]

Chicken is another concern. A baby chick naturally takes four months to grow into a three-pound chicken. Now, with genetic engineering (hormones), it takes six weeks. This creates too much strain on the chicken's internal organs, which means they need medications and antibiotics to survive. When children eat chicken or eggs, these antibiotics get into their systems; so when they get sick and need an antibiotic, their bodies are resistant.[8] Look for hormone-free, antibiotic-free chicken and eggs as well.

Finally, a traditionally healthy alternative, fish, needs a few guidelines. Fresh salmon is my favorite. It contains all the omega acids that your body needs. Wild Alaskan or Atlantic sources are usually the best. I have concerns about farmed salmon because of their diet and the dyes they are given for color. Other nutritious fish are halibut, sardines, cod, and mackerel. Limit consumption of shellfish from contaminated coastline waters, such as bay shrimp and bay scallops. And be cautious of fish that may have mercury content, such as pike, walleye, and tuna.[8a]

What about your busy life, which includes eating fast food and restaurant meals? Well, in moderation, anything works. If you plan to eat burgers, order them without cheese because it is usually the bright orange type, which has artificial dyes in it. Also, skip the fries if they are not real potatoes (some fast-food restaurants use white flour fillers), or if they are cooked in animal fat, not vegetable oil.

Vegetables and Fruits

Today we have three types of produce: organic, conventional, and biotechnically engineered. Organic means no pesticides and rotated soil. Conventional means that farmers have used pesticides and may not have rotated the soil.[9] The new biotech process means that pesticides have not been used topically but are in the seed itself, no rotation of soil, less water used, and scientific changes of the vegetable's DNA.[10] All three are controversial.

I like to buy organic produce whenever I can get to a health food store or find it in my supermarket. Ask your market to carry organic produce. Dark green, red, and yellow vegetables provide the body with the best vitamins and digestive enzymes. Have you ever wondered why it is customary to eat a salad before a big meal? The natural enzymes help you to digest your dinner. I think it is extremely important to eat a lot of vegetables. To eliminate any possible surface germs, wash all produce with a combination of vinegar and water (mixed half and half) in a spray bottle.

Although the food pyramid recommends three to four servings of vegetables and fruits a day, I think it's better to eat six to eight servings of vegetables and only one or two servings of fruit a day. I believe in eating vegetables with all meals. A veggie omelet with organic eggs is a wonderful breakfast. Baby carrots are a great addition to lunch, and a salad or vegetable soup complements a dinner perfectly.

Fruit, on the other hand, should be eaten only between meals. Fruit raises your pH (digestive juices), so you lose a lot of nutrients when you eat fruit with your meals. It is best to eat fruit twenty minutes before a meal or two hours after. This is true for fruit juices for children, too. Give them juice between meals.

Water (Filtered and Bottled)

If you had told me when I was a kid in the 1950s that in the future people would buy water in a bottle and pay a dollar for it, I would have said, "Get out of town!" Sure enough, this is an accepted practice today. Why? Because water has been polluted over the years by pesticides and other toxic chemicals. Water sources are far better than hundreds of years ago, though still problematic in undeveloped areas of the world. Still, many people do not like drinking water right out of the tap, so bottled water has become the trend. You have three choices of bottled water:

- Spring—water from a spring that is filtered

- Reverse osmosis—filtered water, which removes chemicals like chlorine and leaves some minerals; it is healthier and tastes better than tap water

- Distilled—water from a distiller machine that removes all chemicals and minerals; it is considered healthiest and the water has no taste[11]

Many people feel these choices are far better than drinking from a public water supply.

I am also concerned about washing and bathing in water with chemicals and minerals. If you agree with me, you can purchase water-filtering devices for your home. Filtering the water in your home is a gift to your whole family, especially if you are raising small children.

Household Chemicals and Toxins

Cleaning the house can be hazardous, too. Using bleach is good for getting rid of germs, but it produces a toxic smell. You can use toxic-free soap with essential oils like lemon or eucalyptus to wash your clothes. A simple solution of water and vinegar (mixed half and half) in a spray bottle does a great job on almost any surface in the kitchen and bathroom to get rid of bacteria and viruses. It also works on mirrors and, again, does not have the toxic smell of ammonia. You can scour the sinks and tubs with baking soda. If you use traditional bleach or ammonia products, make sure the area is well ventilated. Finally, the most germ-filled item in your home is the dish rag or sponge at your kitchen sink, so be sure it is wrung out and left to dry when not in use. Replace it daily with a clean one.

Vapors from new furniture and carpets can also be harmful to children. Make sure they are aired out before putting them into your house. Chemicals used for dry cleaning are harmful, too. Remove the plastic bags and air your newly dry-cleaned clothes on the porch before bringing them into the house.[12]

Aluminum

Aluminum cookware and foil are another home hazard. When you cook your food in aluminum cookware, the heat melts small traces of aluminum that are ingested into your nervous system. Research studies show that people with Alzheimer's disease have excess aluminum in their brains. Other nervous disorders, like Lou Gehrig's disease and Parkinson's disease, may also be related to aluminum. To be safe, don't drink from aluminum cans. Buy beverages in glass or plastic containers.

Aluminum is also in most brands of baking powder. You can find aluminum-free baking powder at health food stores.

If you check the label on your deodorant, you'll find that aluminum chlorohydrate is almost always the first ingredient. Smelling nice can give your body problems you do not want. There are some alternative products, like Tom's of Maine natural deodorant with aloe, lichen, and coriander. Or my choice, a crystal stick, *www.thecrystal.com*. They both work fine. Preteens and teens need products that keep them smelling nice. Starting them on a natural deodorant is a good habit for a healthier life.

This next piece of research is really upsetting. According to Beatrice Trum Hunter, highly processed and modified milk powder used in some infant feeding formulas has aluminum levels some sixty to eighty times higher than in breast milk. "The high levels are attributed to the use of soy, aluminum-containing additives, manufacturing processes, or storage containers."

If all of this is giving you a stomachache and you reach for an antacid, be sure to read the label because many brands contain aluminum, too.[13]

Dental Care

When your children are ready to brush their teeth, use a fluoride-free toothpaste. Fluoride can have a toxic effect, so, again, try one of the Tom's of Maine products. Even if you teach your children to spit out the paste, they still swallow some. In fact, in 2001, 11,000 children were reported to have had severe reactions to toothpaste with fluoride.[14] Some people tell me that they have to use fluoride toothpaste because their children get too many cavities. Some children even take fluoride pills. If your children are having dental problems, take a close look at their diet. Healthy teeth need calcium. Good food sources containing calcium are organic dairy products, leafy green vegetables, and sardines. If your children do not eat enough of these, calcium supplements may be appropriate.

If your child needs a dental filling, be careful about dental amalgam, which contains silver and mercury. Ask your dentist for a safer alternative. Chewing, drinking hot or cold drinks, and tooth brushing continuously release vapor from the mercury. It enters the blood from the lungs and oral mucous membranes and traverses cell membranes, including the blood-brain barrier and placenta.[15] For a child's optimal health, women should have their mercury fillings removed before getting pregnant and nursing their babies.

Oils and Essential Fatty Acids

Using olive oil for cooking and in salads is good for reducing the risk of heart disease and cancer, as well as for boosting the immune system. Extra- virgin oils should be out on the counter and used by the whole family for optimal health. The advantage of extra-virgin olive oil over other oils is that it has not been refined with solvents but is produced by a cold-press mechanical process. This process preserves the chemical nature of the oil and the natural antioxidants that are needed for the body's response to environmental stress. Studies to back up the benefits of olive oil look at the lower rate of coronary mortality in Mediterranean countries.[16]

Another common oil product is margarine. It is best not to use most brands of margarine because they are made from hydrogenated oils commonly known as trans fats, which have been found to be a major cause of coronary heart disease.[17] Use organic butter if you can get it. It is much more flavorful and is especially nice for baking. Children need good fats to help their nervous systems become myelinated, which calms them down and helps with their vision and learning abilities. Consuming olive oil and organic butter is good for the whole family.

Consider commercial baked goods like crackers, pies, cookies, and pastries with caution and consume sparingly. If you check their ingredients, you may be shocked to learn how many of these products contain hydrogenated oils.

Microwaving Your Food

Heating food in a microwave oven changes its molecular structure.[18] The microwave process causes molecules to vibrate at a higher frequency, and nutrients are lost. It's difficult to totally give up using your microwave oven, because, let's face it, it is convenient. Most of us can live with fewer nutrients, but an even greater concern is microwave cooking in plastic containers. Just like with aluminum cookware, plastic melts when heated, causing us to consume a small amount of plastic. Doing this over many years does not make good sense. Heating formula and milk for babies and young children is of special concern. Infants and toddlers need the most nutrients they can get, and ingesting plastic can't be good for them. Use the microwave oven sparingly for older children and adults. Always use glass or ceramic containers, and warm the baby's food on the stove.

Soda Consumption and Your Bones

It is amazing how many children drink sodas on a regular basis. Most adults are oblivious to the problem of what happens to the body when a soda is consumed. The *American Journal of Clinical*

Nutrition did a study on soda consumption that tested the calcium excretion in urine of adult women. Five hours after consumption, the results suggested that soft drinks containing caffeine were negatively affecting calcium balance. The noncaffeine sodas showed the imbalance to be less. Furthermore, there was no effect twenty-four hours later.[19] This finding indicates that while caffeine soda leaches calcium right out of the bones, it appears that the body is able to adjust by the next day.

This means that it is generally safe for a young child to occasionally consume a small caffeine-free soda. However, sodas that contain a large amount of caffeine should be avoided. Unfortunately, the term in *moderation* does not compute with many people. The result of high soda consumption is "a reduction of bone mineral content as well an increased risk of bone fractures later in life." The problem is not so much the consumption of soda as it is the fact that beverages containing milk and calcium are *not* being consumed.[20]

What's a parent to do? One solution is to give very young children a little noncaffeine soda occasionally. Older children and adults should have no more than one soda a day. Drink lots of bottled water whenever possible, provide hormone-free milk at home, and encourage its use for breakfast and dinner.

Sugar, Artificial Sweeteners, and Natural Alternatives

The large consumption of sugar in this country is pretty obvious. It seems to be in many food products. Although sugar is the culprit of many health problems, artificial sweeteners, namely aspartame and saccharin, appear to be worse.

There is vicious controversy over this topic. Allegations exist that artificial sweeteners are linked to long-term memory loss, headaches, seizures, mood disorders, and brain tumors. Other research claims that disorders such as multiple sclerosis, chronic fatigue syndrome, and diabetes mellitus can be caused by artificial sweeteners.[21] Animal studies point to severe consequences, but a lot of money is made from selling these artificial sweeteners to diabetic consumers and people who just want to have something taste good without the calories. There is no conclusive scientific data that proves that these sweeteners are harmful. Just in case, you should play it safe and not touch the stuff.

Here are some alternatives. Many health practitioners are excited about the herb *stevia*. It is derived from the leaves of a shrub native to Paraguay and Brazil and has been used as a sweetener for centuries by South Americans. It is all natural, free of calories, does not promote tooth decay, and will not elevate blood sugar levels. The Food and Drug Administration (FDA) has not approved it for use in food; however, it may be purchased as a dietary supplement in most health food stores. Get advice from your doctor if you are diabetic and are considering this as a sweet alternative. Other alternatives for nondiabetics are blackstrap molasses; Sucanat, a product made from the juice of pressed sugar cane; barley malt syrup; 100 percent maple syrup; and honey. Look for organic brands of all of these products to insure your safety.[22]

Taking Vitamins

Taking vitamins to supplement your diet is a good idea when you consider all of the controversial points covered so far.

We now know that the most essential concern for the developing child is the brain. Many people already understand the importance of using folic acid to prevent neural-tube defects. This issue has been widely emphasized for prenatal care. However, it seems that more and more children are being diagnosed with Attention-Deficit/Hyperactivity Disorder (ADHD). This condition has been widely treated with central nervous system stimulants, such as Ritalin®, which can cause a myriad of problems. Before turning to medication, it is better to prevent or find the cause of this disorder that afflicts so many children. A deficiency of several essential fatty acids (EFAs) has been observed in some children with ADHD when compared with unaffected children. It seems to me that pregnant and lactating mothers should be taking EFAs, which are polyunsaturated omega-3, -6, and -9 fatty acids commonly found in fish and flaxseed, to prevent ADHD. If nothing else, it will enhance brain functioning, which is a wonderful benefit. Of course, EFA supplements are available. Ask your doctor when your children reach about age two if they can take a supplement on their own for optimal brain and central nervous system development.[23]

To build the immune system, colostrum supplements are available, which simulate nutrients similar to those found in a mother's early breast milk. Cows provide colostrum; however, make sure that the supplement you use comes from cows that are free from hormone injections and that consume organic food. With a doctor's approval, this can be given to babies. Here are some other suggestions from nutrition specialist Mark Alexander:

- *Grape seed extract* for free-radical scavenger antioxidant qualities. This supplement helps to strengthen the cell wall of veins, arteries, and capillaries. It also promotes optical acuity, focusing abilities, and eye health. This can be started around the age of one

- *Ester-C* to build the immune system. It can be started around the age of two

- *A calcium/mineral formula* for optimal bone growth. This, too, can be started around the age of two[24]

Close your eyes and take a deep breath. Visualize your ability to absorb these concerns about the food you eat and keeping your household environment healthy. Know you can achieve these goals for your family. Consider yourself and your children already healthy, whole, and complete. Be grateful for your ability to provide for your family the best that you can.

Chapter Activities

In your workbook you will find the following activities:

- List of unhealthy things you do
- Plan for a healthier life

Now let's move on to the value of traditions for your family.

Sunrise, Sunset
Sunrise, Sunset
Swiftly fly the years
One season following another
Laden with happiness and tears
~ *Fiddler on the Roof*

Grandparents

Holding your first grandchild for the first time is incredible.

You see a little bit of everyone: yourself, the other grandparents, all the aunts, uncles, and parents living now and before you.

You have a sense of immortality, realizing that you will go on and on through the vehicle of your genetic material.

You can just feel your Spirit soaring when you receive that great smile and get that tiny hug.

As the other grandchildren come along, you are amazed at the level of awareness they give you.

The best is when they call you on the phone and tell you about their day.

The best is when they snuggle when sitting on your lap.

The best is when you teach them how to paint and fish and swim and cook.

The best is watching them grow up to be young and strong and so loved by you.

~D. H. Summers

CHAPTER 9

Traditions

Enrichment and Holidays

In our quest to be politically correct, we seem to have forgotten something—the joy that holidays bring to us. I went to a cutting-edge graduate school, Pacific Oaks College in Pasadena, California. It was a beautiful place to learn. I loved the whole experience. While I was attending in the early 1990s, the big emphasis was on a bias-free, no-prejudice curriculum. In fact, the author of the book *Anti-Bias Curriculum: Tools for Empowering Young Children* was one of our professors, Louise Derman-Sparks. At the time, our instructors were extremely focused on this concept of anti-bias curriculum. Holidays were seen as a form of bias or exclusion because of our tendency to stereotype various groups in society. For example, Louise said that celebrating Cinco de Mayo—which is celebrated on May 5 by Mexican Americans, by eating tacos, dressing in costumes, and having a piñata—was a tourist (multicultural) approach to socialization. It was okay, but we could teach inclusion a lot better if we spread the flavor of the culture throughout the year, not just "do it all" on one day. The accepted tourist method of teaching was replaced with a nonbias experience. In other words, many teachers and school districts eliminated holidays so that no one would be offended. As I saw it, the pendulum had swung to the other extreme. By the year 2000 many schools had no holiday celebrations at all.

Many educators and parents mourn the loss of holiday experiences that they enjoyed as children. A lot of teachers and social groups, like churches, agree. Other people are just trying to get an honest grip on how to assimilate holidays. Making sense of universal inclusion without forsaking traditions definitely requires a delicate balance of our social consciousness.

One holiday that has always bothered me is Thanksgiving. The stereotyping of Native American cultures seems to be an injustice. For example, Native Americans are traditionally featured at this time as Indians in full dress wearing headbands with feathers, typical of the plains tribes, along with teepees. The tribes on the northeast coast wore distinctively different dress and did not live in teepees. Having children make headbands with feathers is actually showing disrespect for the Indians' religious practices. Feathers were given only to adults as a badge of honor. Little children did not usually wear them. Also, at this time of year some people sing, "One Little, Two Little, Three Little Indians," which is degrading. What if we were to sing "One Little, Two Little, Three Little Mexicans, or Chinese"? You get the point.

At one time, I partnered with Debra Rains Robinson, the granddaughter of the shaman of the Lakota Nation. She was a classmate of mine at Pacific Oaks. She and I presented workshops in Los Angeles explaining the disrespect that Thanksgiving traditions promoted. At one point I said,"If we were to put a cross in the room and give children small circles to color (representing Holy Communion) and then asked them to glue the colored circles on the cross, that would be disrespectful to Catholics." Debra's response: "Now you're getting it."

It is age appropriate to present Thanksgiving to children six and under as a day of thanks for living in peace and having the blessings that we have in this country. It is about families getting together, enjoying wonderful food and a joyful day. When children are older, at about seven, stories of the first Thanksgiving are better understood. I highly recommend that you read a story about Squanto, the Indian friend of the Pilgrims.

Then there is Halloween. Should children dress up or not? Some people say it's okay as long as they are not really scary. Other people like the Dracula and skeleton costumes. In a sense, you could argue that scary costumes are a viable method to overcome the fears within. Other people dislike the whole notion of Halloween and will not touch it, but they are okay with a fall festival.

What should be done about the holiday issue? An inclusive day-by-day approach is best for all the holidays. As a family, decide how you want to celebrate, but at the same time be sure to teach your children about all the different cultures in the world. You can do this through stories, or you can get dolls and action figures that depict a variety of races, cultures, physical challenges, and gender roles. Also, discuss with your children what stereotyping is. Explain how it is important to make everyone feel welcome and part of your social group.

Louise Derman-Sparks and her ABC task force wanted us to examine our own bias issues. They asked us to search our souls for how we felt about not only culture and race, but also other aspects of society, like classism and homophobia.[2] These are tough areas to explore. When adults are able to model social inclusion, children can follow with respectful appreciation. Parents have different social variables. They can be interracial couples, rich or poor, or gay partners. The bottom line is to respect all parents. Know that their children love them no matter what social category they are from. As parents and caregivers, all you need to do is model respect for your family and school and then honor the decisions of others.

Invent Your Own Traditions

Families do all sorts of things together, such as celebrating birthdays at a favorite restaurant, going to the same vacation spot each year, or having holiday meals together. It sounds so simple. Setting aside time for something that everyone can look forward to doing together makes our busy, hard-working lives tolerable.

My favorite thing to do with our children was what we called Christmas Surprise. Every year we would go to a play, ballet, or concert. One time we went to Disneyland. What made it so fun was that the girls never knew where we were going until we got to our destination. We did this for twenty years each weekend before Christmas, and every experience was a magical treasure.

Something a little more simple was our Sunday morning puppet show. When the girls were between two and six years old, they would get in bed with us. My husband kept a bug puppet under the bed and would use his big toe to give the illusion that Mr. Bed Bug was coming out to greet them. It was the cutest thing. Sometimes even I would believe that Mr. Bed Bug really lived inside our bed with his whole family.

In my preschool class, I had two sock puppets, Susie and Annie. They told the class their problems, and the children helped solve them. It was an effective way to teach socialization and a real part of my personal gift. All teachers and schools have some traditions, like open-house events, a spring carnival, a special closing event for the end of the year. All of these activities are wonderful. Your support honors not only your children, but also those who inherit the traditions.

REFLECTIVE EXERCISE

Close your eyes and take a deep breath. Visualize all of the fun things that are possible to do with your family. Know how wonderful life can be looking forward to having special time with your children. Be grateful for your abilities to enjoy your family.

Chapter Activities

In your workbook you will find the following activities:

- List of traditions you had in your own childhood
- List of your current traditions along with some new ones

Now let's move on to the final chapter about the gifts we give each other.

Grown men may learn from very little children,
for the hearts of little children are pure, and, therefore,
the Great Spirit may show to them many things
which older people miss.
~ *Black Elk*[1]

Immortality

The brightest day is no more useful than the darkest night—
    Our troubles soon would disappear if we'd view them aright.
Good fortune may be holding back her best things to the last,
    For I know that the mill can grind again with water that is past.

And that same little mountain stream
    Has always been to me
But one of Nature's many proofs
    Of Immortality.

~William Tomkins[2]

                       Parenting Outside the Box

CHAPTER 10

Gifts

Positive versus Negative Environment

Consider the following laboratory study. Scientists created two environments for rats: one positive, the other negative. In the positive environment, the rats had fresh water and food, separate rooms with comfortable places to rest, natural lighting, and soft music playing. In the negative environment, the rats had stale or rotten food and water, large rooms without any private areas, rough sandpaper everywhere, bright lights all the time, and loud, unpleasant music playing. After some time, the lab technicians observed playful, loving behavior in the positive environment and fighting and territorial bickering in the negative environment.

We humans are not all that different from the rats in this laboratory study. I believe that an uncluttered and organized home creates a positive environment. At least it's a great goal to work toward. Pleasant evening dinners are also important. I worked hard to create a cheerful and clean home for my family. It was far from perfect—in fact, perfect may not be so good—but it was nice. Our house had only 1,500 square feet, but we felt fortunate with what we had. We didn't necessarily believe that bigger was better. All we really needed was to have our needs met and to live in a pleasant neighborhood.

I had to work at organization because, just like a lot of you, I often found myself in *the land of chaos* (described in Chapter 1). I put a bulletin board for posting notices in the kitchen along with a monthly calendar. We also had a place to put notes to each other. To get everyone to help with chores, I wrote each task that needed to be done on a small piece of paper. I put them in a basket and had the girls draw for work duties. For one whole year we had an exchange student, Michiko, from Japan. The least desired chore at the time was *pooper scooper*, or cleaning up after the dogs in the back yard. We always had a good laugh over who did or didn't get that job. Another way to keep track of chores is to use a whiteboard that lists what everyone needs to do each day. Some families use a star system with an allowance award to encourage children to get their chores done. Your attitude can make all the difference in getting everyone to help out. My mantra was, "Everyone in this family needs to pitch in to make life easier for all of us." Your own success will depend on what quadrant you are parenting from.

Family dinners that provide an opportunity for personal interaction take commitment. Some of my high school students often tell me that the only time they eat dinner with their families is on Thanksgiving, and some of them do not even have that. A great *Reader's Digest* study showed that families committed to eating together on a regular basis had fewer family problems. Children were more likely to graduate from high school and go on to college, as well as have less involvement with drugs, when they had at least three family dinners a week.

This study inspired me to have regular family dinners at my house. I set the table with placemats and cloth napkins. I served food in bowls, which were passed around. Sometimes I put food items in a round tray that spun around, especially when we had tacos. The television was turned off, and no phone calls were allowed. Occasionally we would even have nice music playing and ate by candlelight. When the girls had friends over, they were often surprised by the way we had dinner.

We always started our meals with a prayer, and, most important, our conversation focused on the girls' lives. After fifteen to twenty minutes (if we were lucky), the girls were finished and ready to go about their business; but at least we had fifteen to twenty minutes of quality time. We knew how precious these experiences were because of how fast time passes.

As my daughters became teenagers, it did get more difficult to coordinate our schedules, so we adjusted by having a pot of something like soup, chili, or spaghetti sauce on the stove. We may have eaten in shifts at the counter, but either my husband or I were there to ask how things were going in their lives. In those days, we had our Sunday evening meals together, and that was good, too.

Let us consider what you can do to create a positive environment at the different stages of your family life cycle.

Babies to Preschoolers: Recycle and Simplify Your Toys

Even before a child is born, she starts to collect toys. It begins at the baby shower: rattles, stuffed animals, and busy boxes begin to pour into the house. Toys promote play, which is a good thing. It is not good, however, when the toys become overwhelming. I suggest that you take half of the toys filling the house, especially if your child is very young, and store them in a container in the basement or garage. Every month rotate the toys in the container with those in the house. Every month your child will get excited over the apparently new things. Young children get used to their toys and are easily bored. You'll find this rotation trick works like a charm.

This system also works for older children at home and students in the classroom. Remember, the balance between boredom and stimulation is a delicate one. A good indicator is behavior. When things are ignored, it's time to reach into the storage container and recycle.

Also, even if you have enough money for lots of toys, videos, and other things, be careful. Fitting everything you can into your child's play space can create an overabundant numbness. Simple things like clothespins and a can, old pots and pans, homemade play dough, a patch of "clean" dirt in the yard, or large empty boxes and old blankets to make a fort are all really cool items that stimulate children's imaginations. Keep things simple. Your interest and enthusiasm can make rocks seem exciting.

This homemade play dough recipe worked great for me, especially on rainy days:

---

2 Tbs vegetable oil
2 cups water
2 cups flour
1 cup salt
4 tsp cream of tartar
(Add food coloring and flavoring if you want)
Put all ingredients in a microwave-safe bowl. Stir. Cook on high for one minute. Stir. Repeat five times, or until play dough is thick. Spread dough on the counter sprinkled with a little flour and knead it. Store in an air-tight plastic bag.

Early School Years—Explore Your Community

There is nothing like the gift of first-hand experiences. When my niece, Shayna, was about six, I took her to the zoo. I remember how excited she was to see a real zebra. She said, "I've seen real horses but never one with black and white stripes, except in books." We took a camera with us that day, and I made a special picture book of our day at the zoo, which Shayna loved.

Cognitive learning usually doesn't happen unless there are real-life experiences. Learning is like a pyramid. Figure 11 uses the symbol of a learning pyramid to illustrate an example of a farmer milking a cow. At the top of the pyramid is a small amount of learning, which comes from pictures and books. As we go down

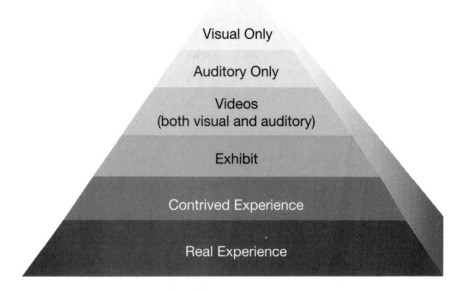

Figure 11. Pyramid for Optimal Learning

the pyramid, a little more understanding comes from audiotapes (such as a cow mooing while the farmer describes the process). In the middle of the pyramid is more in-depth learning through the use of a visual demonstration (such as a video of a real farmer milking a cow). With this example, both visual and auditory senses are stimulated, giving more conceptual information. Finally, an exhibit, such as an artificial, three-dimensional, lifelike farmer figure milking a lifelike cow gets the idea across to children.

I once had a farmer come to show my pre-school class a cow. He did not milk it, but the children enjoyed seeing a real cow close up. I was intrigued with the pyramid concept, so I decided to explore the effect of the next step, a real-life experience.

There was a dairy farm at Mount San Antonio College near our home. One afternoon, my husband and I piled our girls into the van along with all the children from the neighborhood that we could. We learned that the cows were milked at 5 a.m. and 5 p.m., so we were there for the 5 p.m. milking. We witnessed the cows being rounded up and then given a shower so they would be clean. The cows filed into the milking area and were hooked up to machines (so much for the farmer squeezing the udders). Then the farmer pushed a button, and we could see the milk as it went from the cows through some tubes to large silver vats. The farmer explained that the milk was pasteurized, or cooked, in the vats so that it would be good for the children to drink. I tried to explain how the milk in the vats was later put into cartons and driven to the store where we bought it. Only the older ones grasped that part. The point is that this experience was vividly remembered years later. To create the best learning experience, give it as much *reality* as you can. The challenge will stimulate you as well as be a tremendous *gift* to your children.

Visit zoos, museums, tide pools, parks, local theater—anything your community has to offer. It is exciting to witness a beautiful fall leaf or a worm crawling along after a rainstorm. Perhaps you can go for a hike and picnic where you can look down on your town. When you combine both *learning experiences* and *your time*, your children get a double bonus.

Older School Years—The Virtues Within

I love the book *The Family Virtues Guide,* by Linda Kavelin Popov. She says, "A child is a spiritual being who is brought into the world to grow in body, mind, and spirit."[2] Basically, she explores parenting by focusing on fifty-two virtues. She believes that children are born with wonderful attributes; they just need to be reminded and encouraged to practice them. I have been using this concept in both my Sunday school and my secular teaching with great success.

For one year our Sunday school focused on one virtue a week with songs, stories, and creative expression. The children and parents loved it. I have a virtues poster on the wall of my high school child development classroom. At the beginning of the semester I ask my students to introduce themselves by using a virtue to describe who they are. They also write an essay, "My Virtues and What I Plan To Do With Them." I knew this concept had worked when I overheard one of the teenagers say, "Hey, remember your virtue of tolerance." Sometimes I remind them to be compassionate or respectful, again referring to the list of virtues. What better gift can you give your children than the assurance that they have exceptional qualities and are full of potential. To learn about the wonderful programs and materials in The Virtues Project™, log on to *www.virtuesproject.com*.

Long-Lasting Gifts

I started this chapter with a picture of my great, great uncle, William Tomkins, honorary Sioux (Lakota) Indian Chief, because of the gift he gave me. The photo shows him with his friend, Chief Flying Hawk. When I was young, my mom would tell me stories about him. He was famous for writing a book, *Indian Sign Language*. I was fortunate to meet his wife, Gracie, who was ninety-three years young at the time, at their home in San Diego when I was thirteen. Uncle William had already died by then, but it was inspiring to see his house and his Indian headdress.

The gift he gave me was his book. It helped me know who he was without ever having met him. It gives me great pride that his book is still being printed today and is still used by Boy and Girl Scout troops all over the country.

I believe everyone has a book to write, just as I had to write this book. I encourage you to write—not only notes, but journals and stories, too. These writings continue to communicate, even when people pass on. It is a way for your spirit to be recognized when your physical presence is gone.

Notes of Love

Sometimes in our busy world we do not take the time to say, "I love you" or "Thank you." Even though we are all very busy, we need to stop and recognize what is truly important to us. I appreciated my department chair at Mount San Jacinto College, Kathy Turner, who always took the time to write a little personal note on formal stationery. It was her way of making each one of us feel appreciated.

When my daughters were teenagers, the stress of parenting sometimes made me crazy. A friend once suggested that I write positive notes to my girls and put them on their pillows or in their cars. She said that if I thought of something nice to say, they would know that they would make it through whatever crisis was going on at the time. I remember writing a note to Amy. All I could think of at the time that was positive was that her hair was always so nice and pretty, so I wrote her a note telling her this. I did little things like that for both of my daughters, and somehow it helped us get through those challenging years.

You never know how much little things will mean later on. About three years after my husband died, I went through a box of old family greeting cards for birthdays and anniversaries. I cried when I read his brief little messages of "I love you" in his own handwriting. Out of the whole box, I saved a few. One was a birthday note from our oldest daughter, Sharri:

> *Dad,*
> *You look great at 41. People can't believe you're my*
> *father. I am proud to tell them that you're 41 years*
> *old and still look 35. Thank you for all of your talks and*
> *every little bit of advice you give me. I love you for the*
> *little hugs and kisses you sneak in when I get home at*
> *all hours of the night. Happy birthday. I love you.*
> *Sharri*

Another one I saved is from Amy to me:

> *Mom,*
>
> *Just want to thank you again for all that you have given me and all that you have shared. You are truly inspirational to me. Remember how special and loved you are.*
>
> *Love,*
> *Amy*

Extending Yourself to Your Community

The best gift you can give to children and your community is yourself. Volunteering your time as a scout leader, little league coach, dance team driver, or other activity involving children is an opportunity to raise your moral development to Room 3, where everything happens *with me* (as illustrated in Chapter 7). You can get a euphoric feeling when you support not only your own children but also other children in your neighborhood. If they win or lose an event, it does not matter. The important thing is that they tried their best and they know that you loved and supported them. I realize not all coaches are models of positive enlightenment and not all parents are supportive when their child does not win, but most of these experiences have merit. Extracurricular activities promote self-esteem, confidence, creativity, and poise. The payoff is that someday the children you helped will be calm and articulate at a job interview, or convincing and poised giving a presentation in front of clients or colleagues. I am concerned about children who cannot play soccer because of poverty, parents who are too busy, and so on. We can all help with fund-raising so that underprivileged children can participate. Some boys and girls just need a ride to practice. In many communities Boys and Girls Clubs, which provide ample activities, need financial support as well as volunteers.

Recently, my nephew Bobby told me that someone from his Pop Warner football days had approached him. Bobby's dad, Charlie, had been one of the coaches. This old friend asked him to say thanks to Charlie for his support when nobody else cared—it had meant a lot to him. This childhood buddy was not the best athlete on the team. All that mattered was that someone encouraged him and made him feel good for his efforts. Kindness stays in your psyche forever.

Picture Scrapbooks

My last thought on gifts is the art of creating scrapbooks. I find this to be one of the ultimate challenges in our busy lives. I have made only one significant scrapbook, which was of my husband Jim's life. I went to an arts and crafts store and purchased a simple binder with acid-free paper. Then I gathered all of our pictures showing the evolution of his life and spread them out on the dining room table. When I finished the scrapbook, I showed it to my family, thinking I was done. I realized I was wrong when I took a class that taught me I needed more closure. I then wrote Jim's life story, telling of his spiritual journey. It included his interests as a child, the passion he had had for his work and family, how he had found God, and also how he had discovered that God was within him. Then I read it to my classmates for my final project. This was a tremendously releasing exercise. Your time is well spent when you take pictures, organize them so they tell a story, and keep a journal of your life and the lives of ones you love.

REFLECTIVE EXERCISE

Close your eyes and take a deep breath. Visualize all the gifts you give your children every day. Know that little hugs and positive messages are meaningful. Know that you can express love and be loved. Be grateful for your ability to give to your children.

Chapter Activities

In your workbook, you will find the following activities:

- List of the gifts you give your children
- Plan for gifts you will do in the future

On days when you are challenged, in the land of chaos, or anytime you want, here are five steps you can use to connect with your spiritual source:

- Recognize that God is in your life

- Know that a part of our Creator's spirit is within you, guiding you

- Realize that all you want to accomplish in your parenting is already done perfectly

- Give gratitude for your life

- Release your words and trust in God

> *Hi (Your Spiritual Source)*
>
> *I am so glad you are with me today, guiding me on my spiritual journey.*
>
> *I know that my family is secure and that each one is on their right path. I can visualize everything they need for perfect fulfillment and know that it is already accomplished. I release these words with gratitude coming from faith and love.*
>
> *And, so it is.*
>
> *Amen*

May this book be a blessing to you. I will end by sharing my Uncle William's favorite message. Try to picture it with Native American sign language.

"May the Great Mystery make sunrise in your heart."

Notes

CHAPTER 1

1.   Quote from Pablo Picasso.

CHAPTER 2

1.   Briggs, Dorothy Corkille, *Your Child's Self-Esteem*, Dolphin Books, 1975, p 1.
2.   Bradshaw, John, *On the Family*, Health Communication, 1988.
3.   Ginott, Haim G., *Between Parent and Child*, Avon books, 1969, p 109.
4.   Baumrind, Dianne, "Current Pattern of Parental Authority," *Developmental Psychology Monographs*, 1971, (Monograph 1), pp 101–103.
5.   Fulghum, Robert, *All I Really Need to Know I Learned in Kindergarten*, Ballantine Books, 1986, p 184.

CHAPTER 3

1.   Lyrics from "Love and Marriage", Rogers and Hammerstein.
2.   De Angelis, Barbara, *Real Moments*, Dell Publishing, 1994, p 154.
3.   Rosenblat, Lewis and Marge, *Single Parenting* videotape, JUM Productions, 1990.

CHAPTER 4

1.   Quote from Sigmund Freud.
2.   Erikson, E. H., *Childhood and Society*, W. W. Norton and Co., 1963.
3.   Erikson, E. H., *The Life Cycle Completed*, W.W. Norton and Co., 1998.
4.   Axline, Virginia M., *Dibs in Search of Self*, Ballantine Books, 1964.
5.   Munuchin, Salvador, Lecture notes: Sociology 300, California State University at Fullerton, Spring, 1984.
6.   Zukav, Gary, *The Seat of the Soul*, Fireside, 1989, p 139.

CHAPTER 5

1. Ginott, Haim G., *Between Parent and Child*, Avon Books, 1969, p 114.
2. Thomas, A. and S. Chess, *Temperament and Development*, Brunner-Mazel, 1977.
3. Ginott, Haim G., *Between Parent and Child*, Avon Books, 1969, p 39.
4. Hannaford, Carla, *Smart Moves*, Great Oceans, 1995, p 53.
5. Bailey, Becky, *I Love You Rituals*, Harper-Collins, 2000, p 34.

CHAPTER 6

1. Houston, Jean, *Jump Time*, Penguin Putman, 2000, p 73.
2. www. dyslexia.org.
3. Baxter, W., *"Test for Three Types of Learners"* University of the Pacific School of Education, 1974, pp 1–4.
4. Houston, Jean, *Jump Time*, Penguin Putman, 2000, p 81.
5. Press Enterprise, "Chavez Family Sends Five Children to Harvard, June 20, 2002. p 19.
6. Labinowicz, E., *The Piaget Primer: Thinking, Learning, Teaching*, Addison-Wesley, 1980.
7. Golumb, C., and L. McLean, *Perceptual and Motor Skills*, 1964, pp 119–125.
8. Gardner, Howard, *The Unschooled Mind: How Children Think and How Schools Should Teach*, Basic Books, 1991.
9. Hannaford, Carla, *Smart Moves*, Great Ocean, 1995, p 194.
10. Edelman, Marian Wright, *The Measure of Our Success*, Beacon Press, 1992, pp 39–40.

CHAPTER 7

1. Quote from Nelson Mandela.
2. Pitts, Leonard, Jr., " This Teacher Has a Lesson for All of Us," *Detroit Free Press*, June 21, 2002, p 2H.

3. Kohlberg, L., "Stage and Sequence: The Cognitive Developmental Approach to Socialization, in D. S. Goslin (Ed.) *Handbook of Socialization Theory and Research*, Rand McNally, 1969, p 379.

4. Sutton, Marcia, and Lloyd Strom, *The Kingdoms of Creation: A Map of Spiritual Growth*, Nova Tech, 1997.

5. Kubler-Ross, Elizabeth, *On Death and Dying*, Macmillan, 1969.

6. Dass, Ram, *Journey of Awakening*, Bantam, 1990, p 183.

7. Zukav, Gary, *Seat of the Soul*, Fireside, 1989, p 45.

8. Ruiz, Don Miguel, *The Four Agreements*, Amber-Allen, 1997, p 45.

9. Hansen, Warren, *The Next Place*, Waldman House Press, 1997, pp 25–33.

CHAPTER 8

1. Burreson, Rod, *Never, Ever, Ever Give Up*, Norge Publications, 2002, p 7.

2. Sampson, Hugh A., "Peanut Allergy," *New England Journal of Medicine*, April 25, 2002, pp 1294–1298.

3. Sicherer, Scott H., "Clinical Update on Peanut Allergy," *Annals of Allergy, Asthma, and Immunology*, Palatine, April 2002, p 356.

4. Mead, Nathaniel, "Europeans Say No to U.S. Growth Hormones", *Weider Publications*, 1990.

5. Mead, Nathaniel, Ibid.

6. Gillette, Becky, "Doin a Body Good? Studies Link r-GH-produced Milk and Increased Cancer Risk," *Earth Action Network*, 1998, p 42.

7. George, Daniel R., and Daniel M. Sheehan, "Goitrogenic and Estrogentic Activity of Soy Isoflavones," *Environmental Health Perspectives Supplement*, June 2002, p 349.

8. Berkson, D. Lindsey, *Hormone Deception*, Contemporary Books, 2000, pp 220–222.

9. www.howstuffworks.com, "How Organic Food Works," June 26, 2003, p 5.

10. Leahy, Stephen, "Biotech Hope and Hype" *Science*, September 30, 2002.

11. www.freshwatersystems.com.

12. Berkson, D. Lindsey, *Hormone Deception*, Contemporary Books, 2000, p 269.

13. Hunterk, Beatrice Trum, "Aluminum in Food," *Consumer's Research* Magazine, February 1993, pp 8–9.

14. Needleman, Hervert L., and Philip J. Knadrigan, *Raising Children Toxic-Free*, Farrar, Straus and Girouz, 1994, p 84.

15. Berkson, D. Lindsay, *Hormone Deception*, Contemporary Books, 2000, p 128.

16. Stark, Aiza , and Zecharia Madar, "Olive Oil as a Functional Food: Epidemiology and Nutritional Approaches," *Nutrition Reviews*, June 2002, p 171.

17. Deas, Gerald W., "The Bare Facts about Fat," *New You Amsterdam News*, August 20, 1998, p 14.

18. Berkson, D. Lindsey, *Hormone Deception*, Contemporary Books, 2000, p 272.

19. Applegate, Liz, "Soft Drinks: Bad to the Bone?" *IDEA Personal Trainer*, February, 2001, pp 16–18.

20. Ibid.

21. Metcalfe, Ed, Betty Martini, and Mark Gold, "Sweet Talking," *The Ecologist*, June, 2000, p 16.

22. Harris, Mark, "How Sweet It Is" *Earth Action Network*, January 2001, pp 43–45.

23. Burreson, Rod, *Never, Never, Never Give Up*, Norge Publications, 2002, p 59.

24. Alexander, Mark, telephone interview by author, July 2, 2003.

CHAPTER 9

1. "Sunrise, Sunset," Rogers and Hammerstein, *Fiddler on the Roof.*

2. Derman-Sparks, Louise, *Anti-Bias Curriculum: Tools for Empowering Young Children*, National Association for the Education of Young Children, 1990, p 3.

CHAPTER 10

1. Quote from Black Elk.
2. Tompkins, William, *Indian Sign Language*, Dover Publications, 1969, p 107.
3. Popov, Linda Kavelin, *The Family Virtues Guide*, Penguin Books, 1997, p 1.

About the Author

Diane Hawkins Summers has been a child development specialist for over twenty-five years. She started out as a preschool teacher in the Los Angeles County Park and Recreation Department and worked her way up to teacher, training high school and college students. She was a board member of the Southern California Association for the Education of Young Children, Inland Valley for five years. Her specialty was scholarships. After becoming a widow from a thirty-year marriage and raising two daughters, Sharri and Amy Hawkins, she went on to marry Reverend Michael Summers. She and her new husband live in Fallbrook, California. Between the two of them they have eight grandchildren.